Sweaters
for Men

Sweaters for Men

22 Designs from the Scottish Isles

by Alice Starmore

Scottish landscape photography
by Graham Starmore

Fashion photography
by Stephen Aucoin

BALLANTINE BOOKS
NEW YORK

Library of Congress Cataloging-in-Publication Data

Starmore, Alice
    Sweaters for men : 22 designs from the Scottish Isles / by Alice Starmore;
Scottish landscape photography by Graham Starmore;
fashion photography by Stephen Aucoin. — 1st ed.
        p.   cm.
    ISBN 0-345-34534-7
    1. Knitting — Scotland — Patterns. 2. Sweaters. I. Title.
TT819.S35S72   1989   88-92873
746.9′2—dc19

Interior Design and Art Direction by Michaelis/Carpelis Design Associates, Inc.

Manufactured in Japan

First Edition: November 1989
10 9 8 7 6 5 4 3 2 1

To my father, Thomas Matheson

Publishers Acknowledgments

We would like to thank the following for their assistance during the photography shootings for this book: Mrs. Gisela Waterman and the entire staff at Gurney's Inn; Rose Pascale at Foreign and American Car Service, Inc., Shirley, New York; the management at Poxabogue Golf Course, Wainscott, New York; Diane Schacht at B. Altman & Co.; the models, Michael King, Jon Weideman, James Vest, and Gene Carrier in Montauk, and Steven Sands in Central Park; art directors Irene Carpelis and Sylvain Michaelis; stylist Eliette Markhbein and her assistant, Hope; Joanne Di Prima, hair and makeup artist; Judy Schiller; and, of course, Stephen Aucoin, photographer.

Clothing and accessories: B. Altman & Co., New York; Boston Traders, New York; Cole Hahn, New York; Difference International, New York; Orvis, New York; Scandinavian Ski Shop, New York; 1010 Optics, New York.

Contents

Introduction

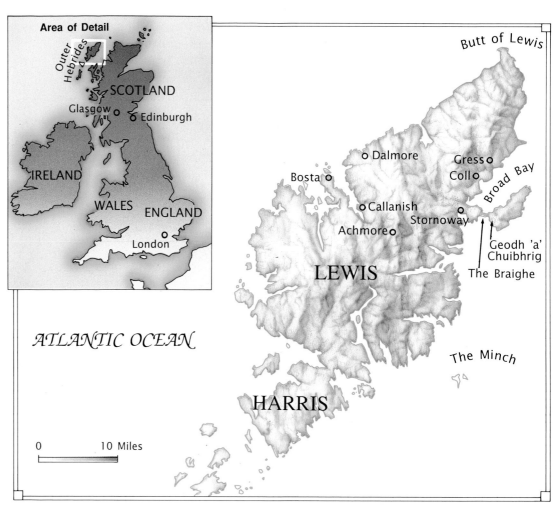

Area of Detail

Outer Hebrides

SCOTLAND

Glasgow   Edinburgh

IRELAND

WALES

ENGLAND

London

ATLANTIC OCEAN

Butt of Lewis

Dalmore   Gress
Bosta   Collo   Broad Bay

Callanish   Stornoway
Achmore   Geodh 'a'
Chuibhrig
LEWIS   The Braighe

The Minch

HARRIS

0   10 Miles

When casting on the first stitches of a sweater, you are taking part in a tradition that owes its origins to the sea. It doesn't matter if you were born just a road's width away from the sea, as I was, or in the middle of Kansas; the fact remains that the modern sweater evolved from the fishing shirt or gansey. This evolution is comparatively recent, for it was only in the 1920s that liberated fashion trends transformed the sweater into a leisure garment for both sexes. Prior to that time, although almost invariably knitted by women, the sweater was a garment for working men—made to withstand heavy weather and hard wear.

In this collection, I deliberately return to that tradition of knitting for men, and my reasons for doing so are partly academic and partly personal. On an objective level, it was both interesting and valid to return to the roots of modern knitting. On a personal level, I was also returning to the factors that started my career as a knitter. I

A croft sheepdog

come from the Isle of Lewis off the northwest coast of Scotland, a Gaelic-speaking community where for generations the two main economic strands have been working the small family farm—called a "croft"—and fishing. The latter occupation has always been hazardous, particularly when

A view into Loch Seaforth, which borders Lewis and Harris.

Shooting the nets on the Home Rule III, *1930s.*

My father, when crew member of the herring drifter Windfall, *Stornoway Harbor, 1930s.*

the boats were small, open, and sail-powered, like the *Home Rule II*, which was owned and worked by my grandfather, Alexander Matheson, in the early part of this century. In the 1920s he joined in a venture with my maternal grandfather, Alexander Macleod, when they became co-owners of the *Home Rule III*, one of the first large vessels to work from Lewis.

My father, Thomas Matheson, started his working life at the age of fourteen on a steam drifter; like all young boys, his first job was that of sea cook, with the additional duty of tending several hundred fathoms of tarred rope. Such young men would be seasoned fishermen by their late teens, and their main quarry at that time was herring. Women worked just as hard, either on the crofts or on the docksides of Scottish fishing ports as itinerant herring packers. Whole families would often be in close proximity as the herring fleet followed the shoals around the coast of Britain: the young fishermen at sea, and their sisters ashore in the packing yards. The season ended in the English port of Great Yarmouth, where photographs often marked the event. Even when working away from

My mother's sister, Ishbel Macleod, and brother Donald Macleod. Studio picture taken in Great Yarmouth, England to mark the end of the herring season.

home, the women knitted—constantly and with prolific output. Men needed working garments, and the women provided them.

I was born in the 1950s, when economic times were easier and occupations had begun to diversify. But to Lewis children of my generation, men putting to sea and women with knitting in their hands were still part of the natural order of things, as was the simple fact that fishermen still wore gansies that were knitted with skill and care. In fact, knitting was an undervalued art, very much taken for granted, and my taking up needles at the age of four was a natural event that needed no comment. It was simply part of a long hand-knitting tradition that was about to suffer a sharp decline as the 1960s saw a trend for mass-produced, fully fashioned garments, and as young people turned away from knitting to other, more modern pastimes.

While returning to tradition, this collection also demonstrates just how far the knitting tradition has come. These sweaters are not only for outdoor wear, but are for the widest variety of occasions. The design process was an ideal opportunity for me to explore yet another personal aspect: how

my work as a designer has been influenced not only by the traditions of the Isle of Lewis, but by its salient visual themes of moorland, mountain, sea, and sky. The low, horizontal landscape of loch, bog, and heather moorland is backed by the overlapping facades of hills carved from the oldest rock in the world. The imagery is subtle but strong, sometimes mournful, sometimes spectacular, depending on light and cloudscape that vary constantly. The hard, metamorphic rock meets the sea at an indented, irregular coastline, producing a combination of sharp, dangerous cliffs and broad beaches of pale sand. Different facets of these features inspired all of the sweaters that follow, and pictures of those natural sources accompany each pattern. After counting up at the end, I discovered that of the 22 different sources of my inspiration, no less than 15 are from the sea or from the shoreline. I certainly did not plan this—it was just the way it turned out. I suppose that road's width must mean something. The sound of the sea has a pervasive echo, and no islander can ever escape its influence.

Sweaters for Men, therefore, has deeply personal roots on a windswept Scottish island at the edge of the Atlantic. However, I am now used to boarding a plane on that island, changing at Glasgow, and looking down over another, somewhat different island—called Manhattan—by the end of the day, and this collection is intended to reflect that in its international appeal. *Sweaters for Men* is firmly based on classic styling and the traditions of knitting, but within that framework, color, pattern, texture, and detail are widely explored. The emphasis is on interest, variety, and enjoyment for knitter and wearer alike, and while the latter was intended to be male, I hope this will not prevent a little "borrowing" by adventurous women. After all, there are few traditions that would benefit more from creative review.

Alice Starmore

Guide to Techniques

GAUGE

Before beginning to knit any of the sweaters in this book, it is absolutely essential to produce the correct gauge using the yarn intended for the garment. This is the only way you can be sure that your sweater will be the size stated in the "Knitted Measurements" sections. The correct gauge is given before the knitting instructions for each sweater. To arrive at the correct gauge, knit a generous swatch (at least 4in[10cm] in width and 4in[10cm] in length unless a specific swatch is asked for) using the yarn, needles, and pattern as specified in the instructions. Bind off the swatch when you have reached the desired length. To calculate the gauge, lay the swatch on a flat surface and pin it down at the edges, being careful not to stretch it. Then, using a firm ruler, measure the *exact* number of stitches to 2in(5cm) at the center of the swatch, then measure the *exact* number of rows in the same way. If the result *exactly* matches the given gauge, you may then proceed to knit the sweater. Remember to count half stitches and half rows—a half stitch in a 2in(5cm) width adds up to ten stitches in a 40in(102cm) width!

If your gauge is incorrect, do not despair. This is not a reflection on the quality of your knitting, and the problem can be solved quite easily. If you have more stitches and rows to 2in(5cm) than that given, use needles one size larger than specified and work another swatch. If this produces still too many stitches, go up one more size, and so on, until you achieve the correct gauge. Conversely, if you have fewer stitches and rows to 2in(5cm) than that given, use needles one size smaller and work another swatch. If necessary, keep trying one size smaller until you achieve the correct gauge.

SUBSTITUTING YARNS

If you have difficulty purchasing the yarn used in any of these sweaters, or if you would prefer to use another yarn, there is one rule you must follow and a couple of guidelines you must consider carefully.

First, the rule: you must achieve the *exact* gauge with the substitute yarn as that given in the sweater's instructions. The needle size used is not important as long as the gauge is correct (see discussion on gauge, above).

You will also need to consider the amount of yarn you will require for the sweater. To do this, consult the yardage given at the beginning of the sweater instructions and compare this with your proposed yarn (remember to make sure to compare them accurately—yards and meters are different, as are grams and ounces). If your substitute yarn has the same yardage, then you should purchase the same amount as given. If your substitute yardage is less than that given, then you will need to purchase more yarn. To calculate how much more you will need, use the following formula:

Yardage given minus substitute yardage
Result multiplied by total amount of yarn given
Result divided by substitute yardage equals extra amount required

The following example shows the formula at work.

Yardage given = 150yds(135m) per 1¾oz(50g).
Substitute yardage = 135yds(122m) per 1¾oz(50g)
Total amount of yarn given = 14 1¾oz(50g) balls

$$150 - 135 = 15$$
$$15 \times 14 = 210$$
$$210 \div 135 = 1 \text{ remainder } 75$$

This example shows that I will need one ball plus seventy-five yards extra. This means, in fact, that I will have to purchase two extra balls to accommodate the seventy-five yards, and I will have a little left over. Any remainder means that you will need to take the result to the next whole number.

The same concept applies if the substitute yardage is more than that given, except that you may need less yarn. The formula is as follows:

Substitute yardage minus given yardage
Result multiplied by total amount of yarn given
Result divided by substitute yardage equals extra amount

The following example shows the formula at work.

Given yardage = 150yds(135m) per 1¾oz(50g)
Substitute yardage = 162yds(146m) per 1¾oz(50g)
Total amount of yarn given = 14 1¾oz(50g) balls

$$162 - 150 = 12$$
$$12 \times 14 = 168$$
$$168 \div 162 = 1 \text{ remainder } 6$$

This result shows that I need one ball less than asked for. Any remainder should be ignored and only the whole figure as it stands should be counted. In this example I would therefore need to purchase thirteen 1¾oz(50g) balls.

Another important consideration is the type of yarn used in the original sweater. If, for example, the yarn is a mohair, then substituting anything else will produce very different results, and achieving the correct gauge will be extremely difficult. I therefore strongly recommend that any substitute yarn be of the same type as specified in the instructions. It is well worth noting that using the same type of yarn in as close a yardage to that given will produce a sweater closest to the original.

FAIR ISLE

This technique uses two colors in the same row or round, stranding the yarn not in immediate use across the back of the work. To strand, knit the required number of stitches in the first color, then strand the second color *loosely* across the back of the work and knit the required stitches in the second color (see fig. 1). The strands should lie flat on the wrong side of the fabric. Make sure that you do not strand tightly, because this will cause the fabric to pucker and render the work useless. On the other hand, the strands should not be so loose that they hang down and risk catching and breaking.

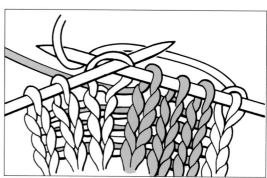

Fig. 1

Reading Charts

Fair Isle, and also some textured patterns, are set out in chart form. Each color or type of stitch is represented by a different symbol on the chart, and a key to the symbols is given alongside the chart.

One square represents one stitch, and one horizontal row of squares represents one row of knitting.

For circular knitting, read all rows of the chart from right to left, starting at the bottom row, and repeat the pattern stitches a specified number of times in each round of knitting.

For flat knitting, start at the bottom row and work the first and every following odd-numbered row from right to left; work the second and every following even-numbered row from left to right. The pattern stitches are repeated a specified number of times across each row of knitting, and the stitches at each side of the marked pattern stitches are worked at the beginning and end of each row.

JACQUARD

The Jacquard technique is best used when the design consists of large areas in different colors. Separate balls or lengths of yarn are used for each area to avoid carrying strands of yarn across long distances. When changing from one color to another, it is vital to cross the yarns to prevent gaps from appearing between each area.

To cross yarns, bring the yarn from the stitches just knitted to the left, on the wrong side of the work. Then pick up the next yarn to be used, bring it under, then over the previous yarn before working the next group of stitches (see fig. 2). Cross the yarns in this manner on every row.

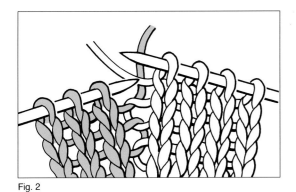
Fig. 2

Bobbins

When working a Jacquard design using several colors at once, make bobbins by cutting pieces of card approximately 3in(8cm) square. Wind several yards(meters) of yarn onto each bobbin. Make a small cut at one

end of each card and slip the yarn through this to stop it from unwinding and becoming tangled with other bobbins when it is not in use.

SWISS DARNING

Swiss darning, also known as duplicate stitch, is embroidery worked on stockinette stitch. It is formed by retracing the original knitted stitches, thus overlaying them with a contrasting color.

To Swiss darn, thread a tapestry needle with the contrasting yarn and bring it through the work from the back, so that it comes out on the right side at the base of the first stitch to be covered. *Then insert the needle from right to left, under the two threads of the stitch immediately above the stitch to be covered (see fig. 3). Then take the needle through to the wrong side at the base of the stitch being covered, and bring it to the right side again at the base of the next stitch to be covered (see fig. 4). Repeat from *.

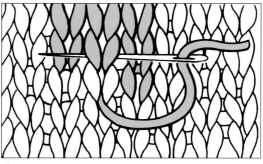
Fig. 3

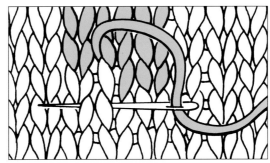
Fig. 4

FINISHING

Blocking and Pressing

Before blocking or pressing, check the instructions on the ball band and also the instructions given in the pattern.

To block, pin out the garment pieces to size, right side down, on a flat, well-padded surface, for example, a large table or the floor covered with blankets and an ironing sheet. Using plenty of pins (approximately 1in(2.5cm) apart), make sure that the stitches and rows are straight, and that the edges are not pulled out of shape. The pieces may either be pressed with an iron or covered with a clean, damp towel and left to dry. If you use an iron, make sure it is at the recommended heat for the type of yarn used (cool for silk, warm for wool, slightly warmer but not hot for cotton). Place a damp cloth over the pieces and press very gently by lifting and setting down the iron. *Do not use a sideways motion.* Remove the cloth after pressing, and remove the pins once the piece has cooled. Do not block or press ribs on the lower edges of garments, or on cuffs and necks, because they are meant to retain their elasticity.

Seaming

For seaming, use a strand of the same yarn or split the ply if it is heavy. For multi-colored garments, use the predominant color. Work small, even stitches so the seams will not gape, but be careful not to seam too tightly, as this will conflict with the natural elasticity of the knitting. Use a loose slip stitch or catch stitch around necklines and in areas where the garment requires some give. Press each seam lightly as you go along, unless otherwise stated.

Abbreviations and Glossary

alt—alternate

approx—approximately

b—back. Knit or purl into the back loop(s) of stitches.

beg—beginning

cm—centimeter(s)

cn—cable needle

dec—decrease

dk—double-knitting

foll—following

g—gram(s)

in—inch(es)

inc—increase

k—knit

k2tog—knit two stitches together

knit up—Insert the point of the right-hand needle from the front to the back of the fabric, one complete stitch in from the edge. Put the yarn under, then over the needle and pull the loop formed on the needle through the fabric quite loosely, and leave it on the needle, thus forming one stitch. This stitch is much like crochet chain stitch.

m1—make one. Knit into the next stitch in the row *below*, then knit into the next stitch itself, thus making one extra stitch.

mm—millimeter(s)

oz—ounce(s)

p—purl

p2tog—purl two stitches together

patt—pattern

psso—pass slip stitch over. Insert the tip of the left-hand needle into the slipped stitch and draw this stitch over the knitted stitch and off the right-hand needle.

p2sso—pass two slipped stitches over. Insert the tip of the left-hand needle into both slipped stitches and pass them over the knitted stitch and off the right-hand needle.

rem—remain(ing)

rep—repeat(ing)

sl—slip. Pass the stitch(es) from the left- to the right-hand needle without knitting or purling.

ssk—slip, slip, knit. Slip the first and second stitches knitwise, one at a time, then insert the tip of the left-hand needle into the fronts of these two stitches, from the left, and knit them from this position.

st st—stockinette stitch

st(s)—stitch(es)

tbl—through back of loop(s)

tog—together

yo—yarn over. Take the yarn over the top of the right-hand needle from front to back once before working the next stitch. This forms a loop over the right-hand needle. The yo is counted and treated as a stitch on the following row.

A note on the rating system:
Each sweater is rated for difficulty from ● (for beginning knitters) to ● ● ● ● (for experienced knitters).

Sweaters
for Men

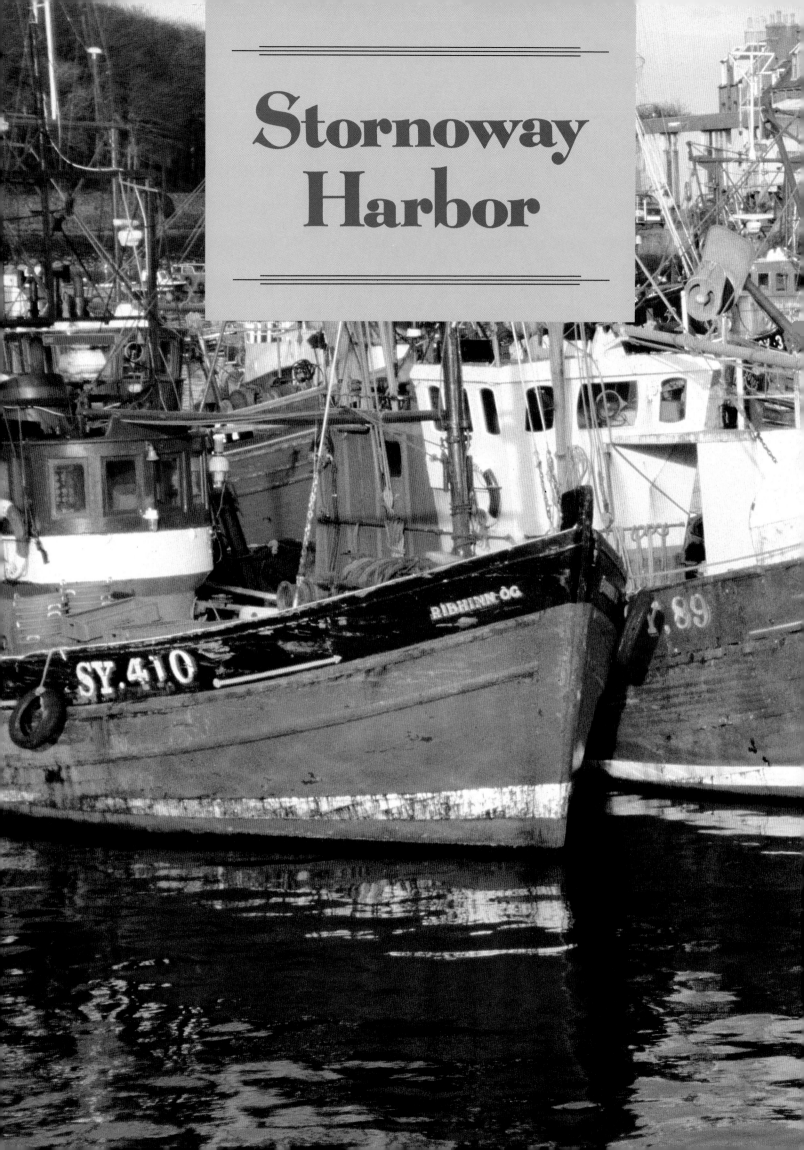

Stornoway Harbor

Gansey Style Sweater

It seems appropriate to start at the quayside of Stornoway Harbor, which has always been the hub of fishing activity in Lewis. It seems equally appropriate to start with a variation on the basic garment in which thousands of fishermen have put to sea. In this fisher gansey, the color, style, and patterns—herringbone diamond and seeding panels—are entirely traditional. Only the small addition of a silk-lined button front and collar takes this out of the realm of the working garment.

RATING ● ● ● ●

Gansey Style Sweater

SIZES
To fit chest 39–41/42–44in (99–104/107–112cm)

KNITTED MEASUREMENTS
Chest 45/48½in (114.5/123.5cm)
Length from top of shoulder 27/28in (68.5/71cm)
Sleeve length 19½/20in (50/51cm)

MATERIALS
Sportweight yarn, 104yds per 1¾oz (94m per 50g):
19/20 1¾oz (50g) balls in navy
1 1¾oz (50g) ball of silk yarn in white
1 set of 4 double-pointed or circular needles in sizes 5 (3¾mm) and 7 (4½mm).
Note: If using a circular needle, sets of short length double-pointed needles will also be required to work the narrow ends of the sleeves.
3 buttons
5 stitch holders
Stitch markers

GAUGE
11 sts and 15 rows to 2in (5cm) measured over st st, using size 7 (4½mm) needles.

BODY
With set of 4 double-pointed or circular size 5 (3¾mm) needles and navy wool, cast on 218/234 sts. Place a marker at beg of round and work k1, p1 rib for 3in (8cm).

Next round—Increase
First size: (m1, k8) 8 times, * m1, k7; rep from * to end of round—248 sts.
Second size: (m1, k6) 4 times, * m1, k7; rep from * to end of round—268 sts.

Both sizes
Place a marker on first and center sts of round (123/133 sts between each marked st). The marked sts are the "seam" sts. Change to size 7 (4½mm) needles and work straight in st st until body measures 13/13½in (33/34.5cm) from beg.

Work gussets
Round 1: k1(seam st), m1, k123/133, m1, k1(seam st), m1, k123/133, m1.

Rounds 2 & 3: knit.
Round 4: k2, m1, k123/133, m1, k3, m1, k123/133, m1, k1.
Rounds 5 & 6: knit.
Round 7: k3, m1, k123/133, m1, k5, m1, k123/133, m1, k2.
Rounds 8 & 9: knit.
Round 10: k4, m1, k123/133, m1, k7, m1, k123/133, m1, k3.
Rounds 11 & 12: knit.
Round 13: k5, m1, k123/133, m1, k9, m1, k123/133, m1, k4.
Rounds 14 & 15: knit.
Round 16: k6, m1, k123/133, m1, k11, m1, k123/133, m1, k5.
Rounds 17 & 18: knit.
Round 19: k7, m1, k123/133, m1, k13, m1, k123/133, m1, k6.
Rounds 20 & 21: knit.
Round 22: k8, m1, k123/133, m1, k15, m1, k123/133, m1, k7.
Rounds 23 & 24: knit.
Round 25: k9, m1, k123/133, m1, k17, m1, k123/133, m1, k8.
Rounds 26 & 27: knit.
Round 28: k10, m1, k123/133, m1, k19, m1, k123/133, m1, k9.
Round 29: knit.

Divide for armholes
K the first 11 sts of gusset and place these sts on a holder; p123/133 sts and place these sts on a spare needle for front; k21 sts of gusset and place these sts on a holder; p123/133 sts for back; k10 rem sts of gusset and place these sts on first holder. Break off yarn.

Back yoke
**With *wrong* side facing, rejoin yarn to the 123/133 sts of back, and work in rows as follows:
Rows 1, 2 & 3: knit.
Rows 4 & 5: purl.

Patt as follows: work **chart A** over the first 16/21 sts; **chart B** over the next 41 sts; **chart C** over the next 9 sts. **Chart B**, reading right-side rows from left to right, over the next 41 sts; **chart D** over the next 16/21 sts.***

Continue in patt as set until armhole measures 9¾/10¼in (25/26cm), with right side facing for next row. Knit 2 rows. Purl 2 rows. Place the center 41/43 sts on a hold-

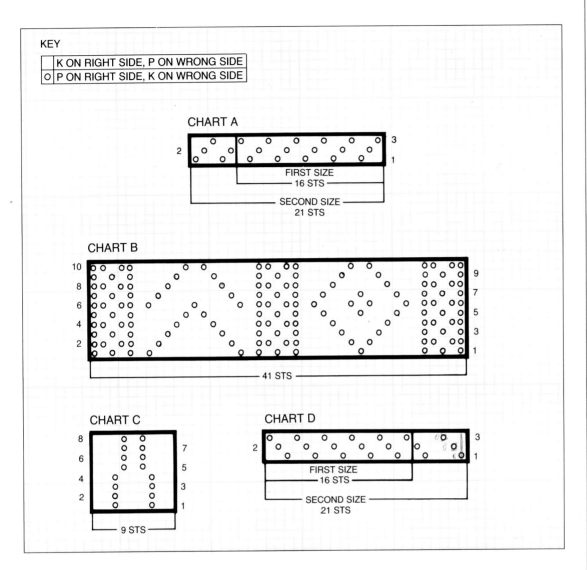

KEY

	K ON RIGHT SIDE, P ON WRONG SIDE
O	P ON RIGHT SIDE, K ON WRONG SIDE

CHART A

FIRST SIZE
— 16 STS —

SECOND SIZE
21 STS

CHART B

— 41 STS —

CHART C

— 9 STS —

CHART D

FIRST SIZE
— 16 STS —

SECOND SIZE
21 STS

er for back neck, and place the 41/45 sts of each shoulder on spare needles.

Front yoke
Work as for back yoke from ** to ***.

Continue in patt as set until armhole measures 3/3½in(8/9cm), with right side facing for next row.

Make front opening and work left front yoke
Keeping continuity, patt the first 57/62 sts; k the next 9 sts (buttonhole band); cast on 1 st; place the rem sts on a spare needle.

Continue working the 57/62 sts of left front in patt as set, and work the 10 sts of buttonhole band in st st, making 3 buttonholes at center of band, the first when opening measures ½in(1cm), the second when opening measures 2¼in(6cm), and the third when opening measures 3¾in(9.5cm). **To**

make buttonhole: bind off 2 sts; on foll row, cast on 2 sts over bound off sts.

Continue to work left front and buttonhole band as set until opening measures 4in(10cm), with wrong side facing for next row.

Shape left neck
†††Bind off the first st; patt the next 16/17 sts and place these sts on a holder; patt the rem 50/54 sts.

Keeping continuity, patt the rem 50/54 sts, decreasing 1 st at neck edge of next and every foll alt row until 41/45 sts rem. Continue straight in patt until front corresponds in length with back at end of chart patts, with right side facing for next row. K 2 rows. P 2 rows. Place sts on a spare needle.††††

Gansey Style Sweater

white silk lined collar e button front

Scottish fleet Pattern yoke.

Right front yoke
With size 7(4½mm) needles, cast on 10 sts for button band; then with right side facing, and keeping continuity of chart patts, work the 57/62 sts of right front—67/72 sts total.

Continue in patt as set and work the 10 sts of button band in st st until right front corresponds in length with left front at top of front opening, with right side facing for next row.

Shape right neck
Work as for left neck from ††† to ††††. Graft or bind off together shoulder sts.

SLEEVES

With set of 4 double-pointed or circular size 7(4½mm) needles, knit up 110/116 sts **evenly** around armhole; pick up and knit the 21 sts of gusset from holder—131/137 sts total.

Rounds 1 & 2: purl sleeve sts and k the 21 gusset sts.

Round 3: knit sleeve sts, then dec gusset as follows: ssk, k17, k2tog.

Continue, working **chart E** over sleeve sts, repeating the 4 patt sts 27/29 times (on first size work last 2 sts as indicated on chart), and knit the gusset sts, decreasing 1 st on each side as set, on every third round until 1 gusset st (sleeve "seam" st) remains.

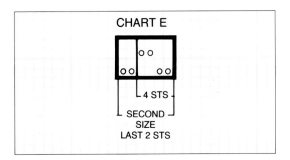

Then continue to dec 1 st as set at each side of the seam st on every fourth round. When sleeve measures 5½in(14cm), cease working chart patt and knit 1 round. Purl 2 rounds, working seam st in knit and continuing to dec as set on every fourth round. Then continue working sleeve in st st and dec as set on every fourth round, until 67/69 sts rem.

Next round—Decrease for cuff

K1/3, *k2tog, k4; rep from * to end of round—56/58 sts.

Change to size 5(3¾mm) needles and k1, p1 rib until sleeve measures 19½/20in(50/51cm). Bind off evenly in rib.

COLLAR AND FACINGS

Collar

With size 7(4½mm) needles and right side facing, pick up and knit 16/17 sts from right neck holder; knit up 19 sts to back neck holder; pick up and knit the 41/43 sts from back neck holder; knit up 19 sts to left front holder; pick up and knit the 16/17 sts from left neck holder—111/115 sts.

Row 1 (wrong side): knit.
Rows 2 & 3: purl.
Row 4: *k1, p1; rep from * to the last st; k1.

Continue in k1, p1 rib as set, and dec 1 st at each end of every row until 89/93 sts rem. Bind off evenly in rib, decreasing 1 st at beg and end of bind off.

Button band facing

With size 5(3¾mm) needles and silk yarn, cast on 12 sts. Work straight in st st until facing corresponds in length with button band from cast-on edge to beg of collar. Place sts on a holder.

Buttonhole band facing

Work as for button band facing with the addition of 3 buttonholes to correspond to buttonholes on buttonhole band. Place sts on a holder.

Collar facing

With right side facing and size 5(3¾mm) needles, knit across the 12 sts of buttonhole band; then cast on 88/90 sts; with right side facing, knit across 12 sts of button band—112/114 sts total.
Row 1: purl.
Row 2: knit.
Rep these 2 rows once more. Then continue in st st and dec 1 st at each end of first and second rows, and work every third row straight, until facing corresponds in length with collar. Bind off all sts and dec 1 st at beg and end of bind off.

FINISHING

With right side of facings and collar together, pin bound-off edge of collar facing to bound-off edge of collar; then continue to pin facing to front edges of collar and along edges of buttonhole and button bands. Stitch facing to collar and front bands all around pinned edges.

Turn facing to inside of collar and front bands and stitch facing around collar pickup line, along inside edge of front bands, and across lower end of bands. Catch stitch facing around buttonholes. Sew on buttons to correspond with buttonholes.

Fair Isle Vest

On Sunday the harbor is quiet and still in contrast to the bustle of the week. A pile of dumped nets caught my eye, and I used their colors for this vest. It has all the ingredients of the Fair Isle tradition, including corrugated ribs and a diced pattern.

RATING ● ● ● ●

Fair Isle Vest

SIZES

To fit chest 37–39/40–42/43–44in (94–99/101–106/109–112cm)

KNITTED MEASUREMENTS

Chest 41/44/47in (104/112/119cm)
Length from top of shoulder
25½/26/26½in (65/66/67cm)

MATERIALS

Shetland 2-ply jumper weight yarn, 150yds per oz (241m per 50g):
4oz (112g) in fawn; 2/2/3oz (56/56/84g) in petrol blue; 2/2/3oz (56/56/84g) in rust; 1/1/2oz (28/28/56g) in blue mix; 1/1/2oz (28/28/56g) in deep coral mix; 1oz (28g) in corn; 1 oz (28g) in green·
Set of 4 double-pointed or circular needles in sizes 2 (2¾mm) and 4 (3½mm). **Note:** If using circular needle, then 2 double-pointed needles in sizes 4 (3½mm) will also be required.
Stitch holders
Safety pin
Stitch markers

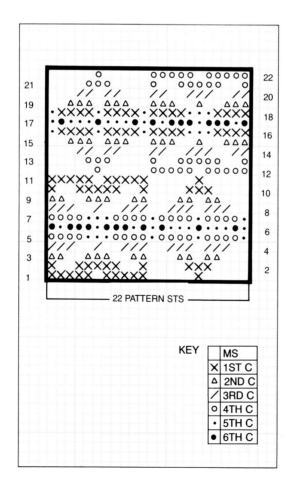

```
21          o     o    o oooo  ooooo    22
19        /// ///       //  ///    //  20
17       ΔΔΔ ΔΔΔ    ΔΔΔ Δ  ΔΔ Δ     18
        •••• •xxxx•xxxx•xxxx• ••xxxx
15       •xxxx •xxxx• •xxxx• •xxxx   16
        ΔΔΔ ΔΔΔ   ΔΔΔ Δ   ΔΔ Δ
13        ooo        o  ooooo  ooooo   14
             o         ooooo ooooo   12
11      xxxxx xxxxx              x
        x    xxxxx      xxx    10
9        ΔΔ  ΔΔΔ  ΔΔ    ΔΔ ΔΔ
        ///  /// ///   /// ///    8
7       ooooo•• •oooo•oooo• •oooo•
        •••••• •••• ••• •••• 6
5       ooooo•• •oooo• •oooo• •oooo•
        ///   / ///  /// ///  4
3        ΔΔ  ΔΔΔ   ΔΔ   ΔΔ ΔΔ
        x   xxxxx xxxx       xxx  2
1       xxxxx  xxxxx       xxx
```

├── 22 PATTERN STS ──┤

KEY	MS
X	1ST C
Δ	2ND C
/	3RD C
o	4TH C
·	5TH C
●	6TH C

GAUGE

15 sts and 15 rows to 2in (5cm) measured over Fair Isle pattern, using size 4 (3½mm) needles.

BODY

With set of 4 double-pointed or circular size 2 (2¾mm) needles and fawn, cast on 280/300/320 sts. Place a marker at beg of round and work colored rib as follows:
Rounds 1 & 2: *k2 in fawn, p2 in petrol blue; rep from * to end of round (remember to bring the yarn to the back of the work after each p2 so that all strands lie on the wrong side).
Rounds 3 & 4: *k2 in fawn; p2 in rust; rep from * to end of round.
Rep these 4 rounds until rib measures 2¾/3/3in (7/8/8cm).

Next round—Increase

With fawn,* m1, k10; rep from * to end of round—308/330/352 sts.

Mark the first st of round. Change to size 4 (3½mm) needles, and joining in and breaking off colors as required, work the patt from **chart**, repeating the 22 patt sts 14/15/16 times in the round. Continue in this manner, repeating the 22 patt rounds until body measures 15in (38cm) from beg.

Divide for armholes

Patt the first 16/11/18 sts of round and place these sts on a holder; patt the next 133/143/151 sts (back); place the rem sts on a spare needle.

Back

Using 2 double-pointed needles, work on right side only, breaking off yarns at end of every row. Keeping continuity of patt, work the 133/143/151 sts of back, decreasing 1 st at each end of next 3/4/5 rows until 127/135/141 sts rem. Patt 1 row straight, then dec 1 st at each end of next and every foll alt row until 107/115/121 sts rem. Continue straight in patt until armhole measures 10½/11/11½in(27/28/29cm).

Keeping continuity of patt, bind off for shoulders as follows: 8/8/9 sts at beg of next 2 rows; 8/9/9 sts at beg of next 2 rows; 8/9/10 sts at beg of next 2 rows. Place the rem 59/63/65 sts on a holder for back neck.

Left front

With right side facing, rejoin appropriate yarns and, keeping continuity of patt, work the next 21/22/25 sts and place these sts on a holder (left underarm); patt the next 66/71/75 sts (left front); place the next st on a safety pin (center front); leave the rem sts on the spare needle.

*Keeping continuity of patt, work the 61/71/75 sts of left front on 2 double-pointed needles, working on right side only, breaking off yarns at end of every row, and shaping as follows:
At armhole edge, dec 1 st on first 3/4/5 rows. Dec 1 st on every foll alt row 10 times. At the same time, dec 1 st at neck edge of first and every full alt row 0/12/14 times, then on every foll third row 23/19/18 times.**

When piece corresponds in length with back, with right side facing for next row, bind off shoulder as back.

Right front

With right side facing, rejoin appropriate yarns and, keeping continuity of patt, work the rem sts from spare needle. Break off yarns and place the last 5/11/7 sts on holder with the first 16/11/18 sts of round (right underarm). With 2 double-pointed needles, work the 66/71/75 sts of right front as for left front from * to **.

When piece corresponds in length with back, with wrong side facing for next row, bind off shoulder as back.

FINISHING

Press garment lightly on wrong side, omitting rib. Sew back and fronts at shoulders.

Armhole ribs

With set of 4 double-pointed or circular size 2(2¾mm) needles and fawn, pick up and knit the 21/22/25 sts from underarm holder, then knit up (into the inside loop of edge st) 151/158/167 sts **evenly** around armhole—172/180/192 sts total in round. Work 10 rounds in colored rib as body. Bind off evenly in fawn.

Neck rib

With set of 4 double-pointed or circular size 2(2¾mm) needles and fawn, knit up 78/82/85 sts **evenly** up right front neck edge; pick up and knit the 59/63/65 sts from back neck holder; knit up 77/81/84 sts **evenly** down left front neck edge; pick up and k the st from safety pin—215/227/235 sts total in round. Mark the beg of round and work rib as follows:
Round 1: *k2 in fawn, p2 in petrol blue; rep from * to the last 3 sts; k1 in fawn; sl next 2 sts purlwise, k the next st in fawn (first st of round), p2sso.
Round 2: k1 in fawn, *p2 in petrol blue, k2 in fawn; rep from * to the last 4 sts; p2 in petrol blue, sl next 2 sts purlwise, k the next st in fawn (first st of round), p2sso.
Round 3: *p2 in rust, k2 in fawn; rep from * to the last 3 sts; p1 in rust, sl next 2 sts purlwise, k the next st in fawn (first st of round), p2sso.
Round 4: p1 in rust, * k2 in fawn, p2 in rust; rep from * to the last 4 sts; k2 in fawn, sl next 2 sts purlwise, k the next st in fawn (first st of round), p2sso. Rep these 4 rounds once more, then work rounds 1 and 2 once again. Bind off evenly in fawn. Darn in all loose ends on wrong side.

Anchor Waistcoat

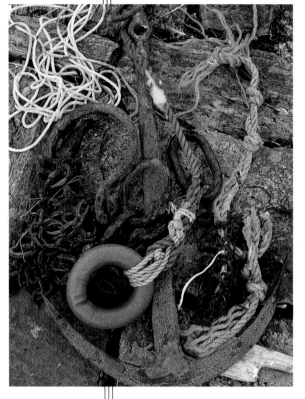

An old, rusty anchor lying in a tangle of nylon rope inspired this new slant on traditional Fair Isle patterns. I used the marvelous colors for the heart-and-wave pattern and knit this in diagonal sections. The yarn is a silk/wool mix, so the result is suitable for more formal occasions. A challenge for the experienced knitter.

RATING ● ● ● ●

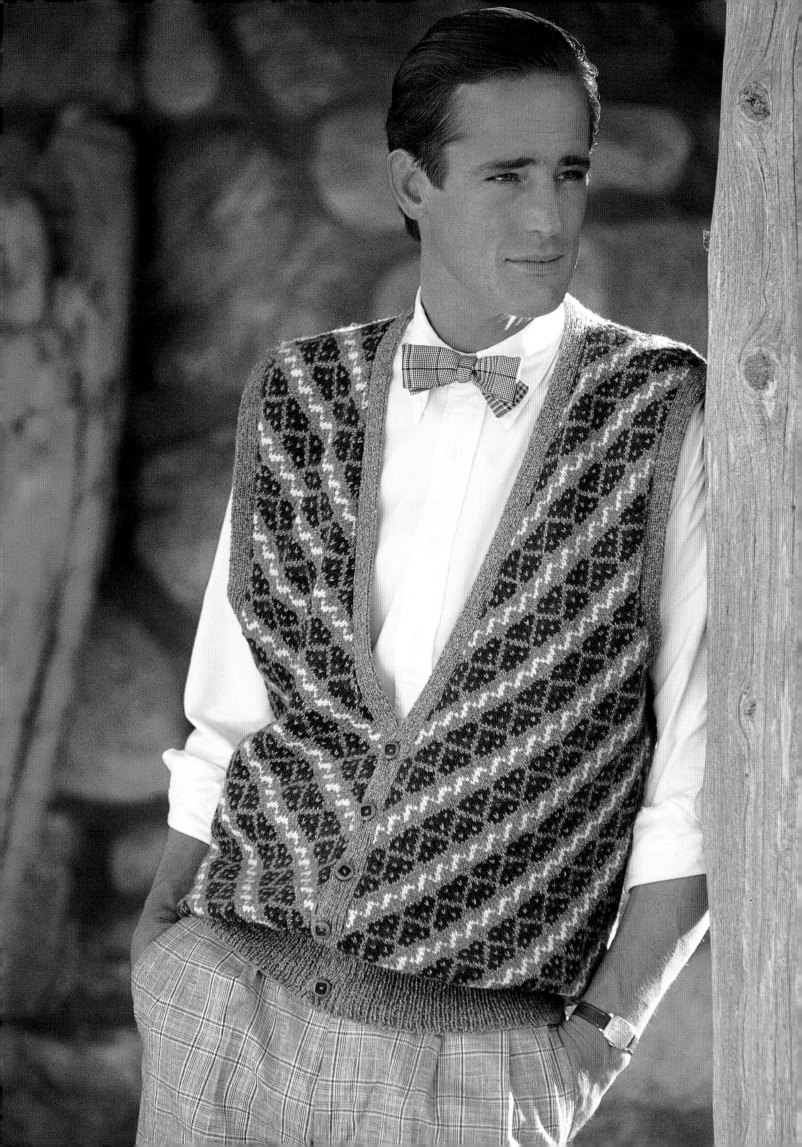

Anchor Waistcoat

SIZES
To fit chest 40–42in(102–107cm)

KNITTED MEASUREMENTS
Chest 45in(115 cm)
Length from top of shoulder 27½in
(70cm)

MATERIALS
Silk/wool mix yarn, 219 yds per 1¾oz
(197m per 50g):
4 1¾oz(50g) hanks in marble; 2 1¾oz
(50g) hanks in blue mist; 1 1¾oz(50g)
hank each of natural, mulled wine, woad,
and chilli
1 pair each size 3(3¼mm) and size 5
(3¾mm) needles
6 buttons

GAUGE
14 sts and 14 rows to 2in(5cm) measured
over patt, using size 5(3¾mm) needles.

RIGHT BACK
**With size 5(3¾mm) needles and blue
mist, cast on 3 sts.

Row 1 (right side, and shown as first row
on chart): k3.

Continue in st st and work from second
row of chart, inc 1 st at **each end** of **every**
row (inc by knitting into the front and back
of the st on right-side rows, and by purling
into the front and back of st on wrong-side
rows). Join in and break off colors as required and work all 39 rows of chart (79
sts on needle). Then continue as set, inc
1 st at each end of every row and repeating
the hearts and wave patterns alternately.
Set the pattern sts of each band directly
above the previous working of the same
patt band, as shown on chart, and work the
extra sts at each side into the patt. Continue in this manner until there are 117 sts on
needle.***

Next row: with right side facing, and keeping continuity of patt, inc 1 st at beg of row
(side seam edge), patt to the last 2 sts,
k2tog (center back seam edge).

†††Keeping continuity of patt, continue as
set, decreasing 1 st at center back seam
edge of **every** row and increasing 1 st at
side seam edge of **every** row until side
seam edge measures 13in(33cm) from beg,
with right side facing for next row.

Shape armhole
Keeping continuity of patt, continue to dec
1 st at center back seam edge of **every** row,
and shape armhole at side seam edge as
follows:

Dec 1 st at side seam edge of next 6 rows.
Work armhole edge straight for 1 row, then
dec 1 st at same edge of next row. Rep
these last 2 rows once more. Work armhole
edge straight for 16 rows—83 sts rem.

Then, keeping continuity of patt, continue
to dec 1 st on **every** row at center back
seam, and inc 1 st on **every** row at armhole
edge, and continue in this manner until
armhole measures 11½in(29cm), with
right side facing for next row.

Shape top
Continue to dec 1 st on **every** row at center back seam, and keeping continuity of
patt, shape top at armhole edge as follows:

Dec 1 st at armhole edge of next 6 rows.
Work armhole edge straight for 1 row. Rep
these last 7 rows twice more. Then continue to dec 1 st at each end of **every** row until 2 sts rem. K2tog and fasten off.††††

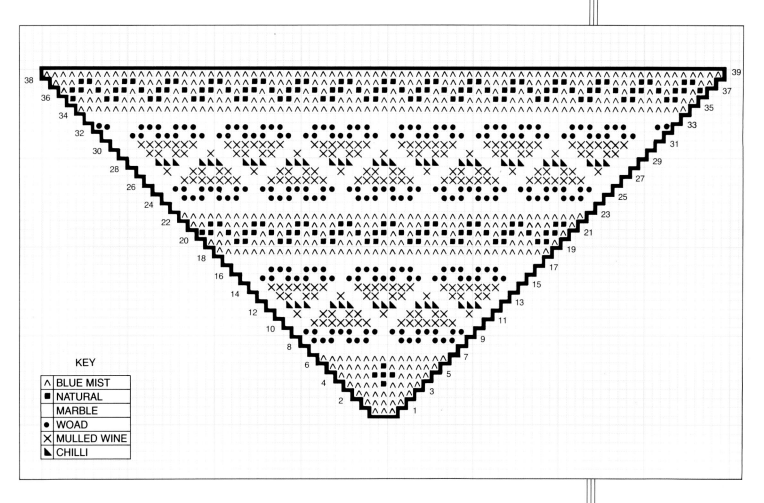

KEY

∧	BLUE MIST
■	NATURAL
	MARBLE
●	WOAD
✕	MULLED WINE
◤	CHILLI

LEFT BACK

Work as for right back from ** to ***.

Next row: with right side facing, and keeping continuity of patt, dec 1 st at beg of row (center back seam edge), patt to the last st and inc on this st (side seam edge).

Then work as for right back from ††† to ††††, but reading "with **wrong** side facing for next row" before working armhole shaping and top shaping.

LEFT FRONT

Work as for right back from ** to ***

Next row: with right side facing, and keeping continuity of patt, inc 1 st at beg of row (side seam edge), patt to the last 2 sts, k2tog (center front edge).

Keeping continuity of patt, continue in this manner, decreasing 1 st at center front edge of **every** row, and continue to inc 1 st at side seam edge of **every** row until side seam edge measures 13in(33cm) from beg, with right side facing for next row.

Continue to dec 1 st at center front edge of every row and shape armhole at side seam edge, as given for right back. Then continue to inc 1 st at armhole edge of every row and dec at center front edge of every row until center front seam measures 10in (25.5cm) from beg, with right side facing for next row.

Anchor
Waistcoat

Diagonal knit Fair Isle Pattern.

Shape front neck
Row 1: inc 1 st at armhole edge as set, patt to the last 4 sts; k2tog twice.
Row 2: dec 1 st at center front edge, patt to the last st and inc on this st as set.

Continue to inc 1 st at armhole edge of every row and continue to dec as set for neck shaping until armhole corresponds in length with that of back, with right side facing for next row.

Shape top
Continue to dec at neck edge as set and dec 1 st at armhole edge of next 6 rows. Work straight at armhole edge for 1 row. Repeat these last 7 rows twice more. Dec 1 st at each end of every row until 2 sts rem. K2tog and fasten off.

RIGHT FRONT
Work as for right back from ** to ***.

Next row: with right side facing, and keeping continuity of patt, dec 1 st at beg of row (center front edge), patt to the last st and inc on this st (side seam edge).

Then work as for left front but reversing shapings.

FINISHING
Press all pieces very lightly on wrong side. Sew right and left back together at center back seam. Press seam on wrong side.

Back rib
With right side facing, and size 3(3¼mm) needles and marble, knit up 128 sts along lower edge of back. K1, p1 rib for 3in(8cm). Bind off evenly in rib.

Left front rib
With right side facing, and size 3(3¼mm) needles and marble, knit up 64 sts along lower edge of left front. K1, p1 rib for 3in(8cm). Bind off evenly in rib.

Right front rib
Work as for left.

Sew back and fronts together at shoulder seams. Press seams on wrong side.

Armhole bands (make 2)
With size 3(3¼mm) needles and marble, cast on 11 sts.
Row 1: k2,(p1, k1) 4 times, k1.
Row 2: *k1, p1; rep from * to the last st; k1.
Rep these 2 rows until bands fit along armholes when slightly stretched. Sew in position as you go along.

Sew up side seams, and press seams on wrong side, omitting ribs.

Button band
With size 3(3¼mm) needles and marble, cast on 11 sts. Work as for armhole bands, until band fits along right front from lower edge to center back neck when slightly stretched. Sew in position as you go along. With contrasting yarn or safety pins, mark position of 6 buttons, the first ½in(1cm) from lower edge, the last at beg of neck shaping, and the remainder spaced evenly between.

Buttonhole band
Work as for button band, with the addition of 6 buttonholes to correspond with button positions on button band. (**To make buttonhole:** Rib 4, bind off 3, rib 4. On foll row, cast on 3 sts over bound off sts.) Sew buttonhole band in position along left front as you go along. Sew on buttons to correspond with buttonholes.

Boat and Rope Sweater

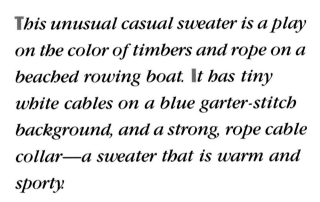

This unusual casual sweater is a play on the color of timbers and rope on a beached rowing boat. It has tiny white cables on a blue garter-stitch background, and a strong, rope cable collar—a sweater that is warm and sporty.

RATING ● ● ●

Boat and Rope Sweater

SIZES
To fit chest
38/40/42/44in(97/102/107/112cm)

KNITTED MEASUREMENTS
Chest 45/48/50½/53in
(113/120/126/133cm)
Length from top of shoulder
26½/27/27½/28in(67.5/68.5/70/71cm)
Sleeve length 19/19½/19½/20in
(48.5/49.5/49.5/51cm)

MATERIALS
Shetland 3-ply yarn, 170yds per 2oz(139m
per 50g):
4/5/5/5 2oz(50g) hanks in white; 5/5/6/6
2oz(50g) hanks in pale blue; 2/2/2/3
2oz(50g) hanks in bright blue
1 pair each size 4(3½mm), size 7(4½mm),
and size 9(5½mm) needles
1 cable needle

GAUGE
Work a gauge swatch as follows: with size
7(4½mm) needles and white, cast on 22
sts. Join in colors as required and work 20
rows in patt as for back. Bind off all sts. The
finished swatch should measure 3⅝in
(9.7cm) in width and 2in(5cm) in length.

BACK
With size 4(3½mm) needles and pale blue,
cast on 116/122/128/136 sts. K1, p1 rib,
working 4 rows pale blue and 2 rows bright
blue alternately until rib measures
3in(8cm).

Next row—Increase
Rib 7/4/1/5, *m1, rib 6; rep from * to the
last 7/4/1/5 sts; m1, rib 7/4/1/5—134/142/
150/158 sts.

Change to size 7(4½mm) needles and,
joining in colors as required, patt as
follows:
Row 1 (right side): with white, sl1
knitwise; k to end of row.
Row 2: with white, sl1 knitwise; p to end
of row.
Row 3: with pale blue, sl1 knitwise; *p4,
sl4 purlwise with yarn at back; rep from *
to the last 5 sts; p4, k1.

Row 4: with pale blue, sl1 knitwise; *k4, sl4
purlwise with yarn at front; rep from * to
the last 5 sts; k5.
Row 5: with white, sl1 knitwise; *k4, sl 2
sts to cn and hold at back, k2, then k2 from
cn; rep from * to the last 5 sts; k5.
Row 6: with white, as row 2.
Row 7: with pale blue, as row 3.
Row 8: with bright blue, as row 4.
Rows 9 & 10: with white, as rows 1 & 2.
Row 11: with bright blue, as row 3.
Row 12: with pale blue, as row 4.
Rows 13 & 14: with white, as rows 5 & 6
Rows 15 & 16: with pale blue, as rows 3 &
4.

Rep rows 1 through 16 until back measures
26½/27/27½/28in(67.5/68.5/70/71cm)
from beg, with right side facing for next
row.

Shape Shoulders
Keeping continuity of patt, bind off
11/11/12/13 sts at beg of next 2 rows. Bind
off 11/12/12/13 sts at beg of next 2 rows.
Bind off 11/12/13/13 sts at beg of next 4
rows. Bind off the rem 46/48/50/54 sts for
back neck.

FRONT
Work as for back until front measures
24¼/24¾/25¼/25½in(61.5/63/64/65cm)
from beg, with right side facing for next
row.

Shape left neck
Patt 55/58/61/64 sts; place the rem sts on a
spare needle. Keeping continuity of patt,
turn and work these first 55/58/61/64 sts,
decreasing 1 st at beg (neck edge) of first
and every foll alt row 11/11/11/12 times.
When front corresponds in length with
back at beg of shoulder shaping, with right
side facing for next row, shape shoulder as
follows:

††Bind off 11/11/12/13 sts at beg of next row. Patt 1 row straight.

Bind off 11/12/12/13 sts at beg of next row. Patt 1 row straight. Bind off 11/12/13/13 sts at beg of next row. Patt 1 row straight. Bind off the rem 11/12/13/13 sts.†††

Bind off front neck and shape right neck

With right side facing, rejoin appropriate colors and bind off the next 24/26/28/30 sts (center front) from spare needle; then, keeping continuity, patt the rem 55/58/61/64 sts from spare needle. Turn, and keeping continuity, patt these sts, decreasing 1 st at neck edge of next and every foll alt row 11/11/11/12 times. When front corresponds in length with back at beg of shoulder shaping, with wrong side facing for next row, shape shoulder as for left from †† to †††.

SLEEVES

With size 4(3½mm) needles and pale blue, cast on 54/58/60/62 sts. K1, p1 rib as back for 2¾in(7cm).

Next row—Increase

Rib 2/1/3/3, *m1, rib 7/5/6/8; rep from * to the last 2/1/3/3 sts; m1, rib 2/1/3/3—62/70/70/70 sts.

Change to size 7(4½mm) needles and, joining in colors as required, patt as back, increasing 1 st at each end of third/ninth/fifth/third row, and thereafter at each end of every fifth row until there are 126/132/134/138 sts in total. Work all increased sts into patt (working white cable sts straight in st st until there are 4, then cable). Continue straight in patt until sleeve measures 19/19½/19½/20in(48.5/49.5/49.5/51cm) from beg, ending with right side facing for next row. Bind off all sts.

FINISHING

Sew back and front together at shoulders. Press seams lightly on the wrong side.

Collar

With size 9(5½mm) needles and 2 strands of white, cast on 26 sts. Patt as follows:
Row 1 (wrong side): k2, *p6, k2; rep from * to end of row.
Row 2: p2, *k6, p2; rep from * to end of row.
Row 3 & all wrong-side rows: as row 1.
Row 4: p2, * sl next 3 sts to cn and hold at front, k3, then k3 from cn, p2; rep from * to end of row.
Row 6: as row 2.
Rep rows 1 through 6 until collar fits lengthwise around neck. Bind off all sts.

With right sides of collar and garment facing each other, place cast-on end of collar at right shoulder seam. Pin, then stitch collar along back neck and around front neck so that bound-off end of collar meets the cast-on end at right shoulder seam. Sew up collar at bound-off/cast-on seam. Turn collar in half to the inside and slip stitch in position around neckline.

Place center top of sleeves at shoulder seams and sew sleeves to body. Press seams lightly on the wrong side. Sew up side and sleeve seams. Press seams lightly on the wrong side.

Broad
Bay

Classic Cardigan

Broad Bay is a sheltered stretch of sea to the north of Stornoway, and its western shore has wide beaches, backed by a strip of sandy coastal land, known as machair, *that is famed for its wildflowers.* **T**he colors of sea, sand, grasses, clover, and vetch are all present in this impressionistic interpretation of the machair *in summer.* **A**n easy style with subtle, textured stripes, this cardigan's flecks of bright color come from a suitably speckled yarn.

RATING ● ●

Classic Cardigan

SIZES
To fit chest 38/40/42/44in
(97/102/107/112cm)

KNITTED MEASUREMENTS
Chest 44½/46½/48½/50½in
(113/118/123/128cm)
Length from top of shoulder
26½/27/27½/28in(67.5/68.5/70/71cm)
Sleeve length (cuff to underarm)
19/19¼/19¾/20in(48/49/50/51cm)

MATERIALS.
Lightweight yarn, 138 yds per oz(112.5m
per 25g): 6/6/7/7oz(175/175/200/200g) in
dark green fleck; 7/7/8/8oz(200/200/225/
225g) in soft green fleck; 6/6/6/7oz
(175/175/175/200g) in blue fleck;
7/7/8/8oz(200/200/225/225g) in
gray fleck
1 pair each size 4(3½mm) and size
6(4mm) needles
1 stitch holder
9 buttons

GAUGE
12 sts and 15 rows to 2in(5cm) measured
over moss stitch patt, using 2 strands of
yarn together and size 6(4mm) needles.

BACK
With size 4(3½mm) needles and 2 strands
of dark green, cast on 112/118/122/128 sts.
K1, p1 rib in color sequence as follows:

* 2 rows of 2 strands dark green / 2 rows of
1 strand dark green and 1 strand soft green
/ 2 rows of 2 strands soft green / 2 rows of 1
strand soft green and 1 strand gray / 2 rows
of 2 strands gray / 2 rows of 1 strand gray
and 1 strand blue / 2 rows of 2 strands blue
/ 2 rows of 1 strand blue and 1 strand dark
green / 2 rows of 2 strands dark green / 2·
rows of 1 strand dark green and 1 strand
blue / 2 rows of 2 strands blue / 2 rows of 1
strand blue and 1 strand gray / 2 rows of 2
strands gray / 2 rows of 1 strand gray and 1
strand soft green / 2 rows of 2 strands soft
green / 2 rows of 1 strand soft green and 1
strand dark green; rep from* until rib measures 3in(8cm), with second row of stripe
to be worked on next row.

Next row—Increase
Continue in color sequence as set and rib
3/6/3/6, * m1, rib 5; rep from * to the last
4/7/4/7 sts; m1, rib 4/7/4/7—134/140/146/
152 sts.

Change to size 6(4mm) needles and continue working in color sequence as set and
work moss stitch as follows:
Rows 1 & 2: *k1, p1; rep from * to end
of row.
Rows 3 & 4: *p1, k1; rep from * to end
of row.

Rep these 4 rows, working in color sequence as set, until back measures
16/16¼/16½/16¾in(41/41.5/42/42.5cm)
from beg.

Shape armholes
Keeping continuity of patt and color
sequence, bind off 3 sts at beg of next 2
rows. Bind off 2 sts at beg of next 2 rows.
Dec 1 st at each end of next row. Patt 1 row
straight, then dec 1 st at each end of next
and foll alt row—118/124/130/136 sts rem.

Continue straight in patt and color sequence until armhole measures
10½/10¾/11/11¼in(27/27.5/28/28.5cm).

Shape shoulders and neck
Keeping continuity of patt and color sequence, bind off 12/12/13/14 sts, patt the
next 27/29/30/31 sts; place the next
40/42/44/46 sts on a holder (back neck);
place the rem sts on a spare needle. Turn
and work first shoulder as follows:
K2tog, patt to end of row.
Next row: bind off 12/13/13/14 sts; patt to
the last 2 sts; k2tog.
Next row: k2tog, patt to end of row.
Bind off the rem 12/13/14/14 sts.

slightly
shaded
armhole.

4 color
shaded
moss st.

1x1 striped
ribs.

Classic Cardigan

Keeping continuity of patt and color sequence, rejoin appropriate yarns to the sts on spare needle and beg at neck edge, patt to end of row.

Next row: bind off 12/12/13/14 sts, patt to end of row.

Next row: k2tog, patt to end of row.

Next row: bind off 12/13/13/14 sts, patt to the last 2 sts; k2tog.

Next row: k2tog, patt to end of row. Bind off the rem 12/13/14/14 sts.

FRONT (MAKE 2)

With size 4(3½mm) needles and 2 strands of dark green, cast on 54/56/58/60 sts. K1, p1 rib in color sequence as for back for 3in(8cm), ending with second row of stripe to be worked on next row.

Next row—Increase

Continue in color sequence and rib 4/5/1/2, *m1, rib 5; rep from * to the last 5/6/2/3 sts; m1, rib 5/6/2/3—64/66/70/72 sts.

Change to size 6(4mm) needles and continue in color sequence as set, and work moss stitch as for back until front measures 15/15¼/15½/15¾in(38/39/39.5/40cm), with second row of color stripe to be worked on next row.

Shape V neck

Keeping continuity of patt, dec 1 st at beg of next row. Then dec 1 st at **same** edge of every foll fourth row. When front corresponds in length with back at beg of armhole, **continue decreasing 1 st at neck edge of every fourth row** and shape armhole edge as follows:

Bind off 3 sts, patt to end of row.
Patt 1 row.
Next row: bind off 2 sts, patt to end of row.
Patt 1 row.
Next row: k2tog, patt to end of row.
Rep the last 2 rows 2 more times.

Continue straight at armhole edge and continue to dec 1 st at neck edge of every fourth row until 36/38/40/42 sts rem. Continue straight in patt until armhole corresponds in length with that of back, with armhole edge at beg of next row.

Shape shoulder

Keeping continuity of patt and color sequence, bind off 12/12/13/14 sts, patt to end of row. Patt 1 row straight. Bind off 12/13/13/14 sts, patt to end of row. Patt 1 row straight. Bind off the rem 12/13/14/14 sts.

SLEEVES

With size 4(3½mm) needles and 2 strands of dark green, cast on 60/62/64/66 sts. K1, p1 rib in color sequence as for back for 3in(8cm), ending with second row of stripe to be worked on next row.

Next row—Increase

Continue in color sequence and rib 2/3/4/5, *m1, rib 5; rep from * to the last 3/4/5/6 sts; m1, rib 3/4/5/6—72/74/76/78 sts.

Change to size 6(4mm) needles and continue working in color sequence as set and work moss stitch for 8 rows.

Keeping continuity of patt and color sequence, inc 1 st at each end of next and every foll fourth row until there are 126/128/132/134 sts in total. Continue straight in patt and color sequence until sleeve measures 19/19¼/19¾/20in(48/49/50/51cm) from beg.

Shape top

Keeping continuity of patt and color sequence, bind off 4 sts at beg of next 6 rows. Then bind off 6 sts at beg of next 4 rows. Bind off the rem sts.

FINISHING

Do not press garment pieces. Sew back and fronts together at shoulder seams.

Place center top of sleeves at shoulder seams and sew sleeves into armholes. Press all seams very lightly on wrong side. Sew up side and sleeve seams. Press seams very lightly on wrong side, omitting ribs.

Button band

With right side facing, size 4(3½mm) needles, and 1 strand blue and 1 strand gray, knit up 180/183/186/189 sts along right front opening, from cast-on edge to top of shoulder; knit up 4 sts to back neck holder; pick up and knit the first 20/21/22/23 sts from back neck holder—204/208/212/216 sts.

K1, p1 rib as follows: 2 rows of 2 strands gray / 2 rows of 1 strand gray and 1 strand soft green / 2 rows of 2 strands soft green / 2 rows of 1 strand soft green and 1 strand dark green / 2 rows of 2 strands dark green. With dark green, bind off evenly in rib.

With contrasting yarn or safety pins, mark position of buttons on button band, the first ½in(1cm) from lower edge, the last at beg of V shaping, and the remainder spaced evenly between.

Buttonhole band

With needles and colors as for button band, and right side facing, pick up and knit the rem sts from back neck holder; knit up 4 sts to shoulder seam; knit up 180/183/186/189 sts to cast-on edge—204/208/212/216 sts. K1, p1 rib in color sequence as button band. On fifth row make buttonholes to correspond with button positions on button band. (**To make buttonholes:** on fifth row, bind off 2 sts for each buttonhole. On foll row cast on 2 sts over bound-off sts.)

Sew up center back neck rib seam. Sew on buttons.

Sand Rib Vest

As the tide goes out, the gently shelving sand around Broad Bay is left ridged and rippled by the retreating water. **I** took both the sand's color and its ridged texture for this simple, classic vest in elegant knit and purl sand stitch. **A**gain, the use of a silk/ wool yarn gives this vest the finish for smart occasions.

RATING ●

Sand Ribbed Vest

SIZES
To fit chest
38/40/42/44in(97/102/107/112cm)

KNITTED MEASUREMENTS
Chest 40½/43/45/47in
(104/109.5/114.5/119.5cm)
Length from top of shoulder
25½/26/26½/27in(65/66/67.5/69cm)

MATERIALS
Silk/wool yarn, 132yds per 1¾oz(121/m
per 50g): 7/7/7/8 1¾oz(50g) balls in
cream

1 pair each size 5(3¾mm) and size 7
(4½mm) needles

GAUGE
11 sts and 14 rows to 2in(5cm) measured
over patt, using size 7(4½mm) needles. To
work a gauge swatch, cast on 21 sts and
patt as for back. Block swatch flat and measure gauge.

BACK
With size 5(3¾mm) needles, cast on
98/102/108/112 sts. K1, p1 rib for 2¾in
(7cm).

Next row—Increase
Rib 1/2/5/8, *m1, rib 8/7/7/6; rep from * to
the last 1/2/5/8 sts; m1, rib 1/2/5/8—111/
117/123/129 sts.

Change to size 7(4½mm) needles and patt
as follows:
Row 1 (right side):*p3, k1, p1, k1; rep
from * to the last 3 sts; p3.
Row 2: *k3, p3; rep from * to the last 3 sts;
k3.††
Rep these 2 rows until back measures
15¾/16/16/16in(40/41/41/41cm) from
beg, with right side facing for next row.

Shape armholes
Keeping continuity of patt, bind off 7 sts at
beg of next 2 rows. Bind off 2 sts at beg of
next 2 rows. Dec 1 st at each end of next 6
rows. Patt 1 row straight. Dec 1 st at each
end of next and every foll alt row until
73/77/81/85 sts rem.

Continue straight in patt until armhole
measures 9¾/10/10½/11in(25/25.5/27/
28cm), with right side facing for next row.

Shape shoulders
Keeping continuity of patt, bind off 6/6/7/7
sts at beg of next 4 rows. Bind off 7/8/7/8
sts at beg of next 2 rows. Bind off the rem
35/37/39/41 sts for back neck.

FRONT
Work as for back to ††.
Rep the 2 patt rows until front measures
14½/14¾/14¾/14¾in(37/37.5/37.5/
37.5cm) from beg, with right side facing
for next row.

Divide for V neck
Patt 55/58/61/64 sts; place the rem sts on a
spare needle.

Left front

Turn, and keeping continuity of patt, dec 1 st at beg (neck edge) of next and every foll fourth row. When left front corresponds in length with back at beg of armhole shaping, and with right side facing for next row, continue to dec at neck edge on every fourth row and shape armhole as follows:

***Bind off 7 sts at beg (armhole edge) of next row. Patt 1 row, then bind off 2 sts at beg (armhole edge) of next row. Dec 1 st at armhole edge of next 3 rows. Patt 1 row, then dec 1 st at armhole edge of next and every foll alt row 7/8/9/10 times (check with back armhole—all shaping should match and finish on same patt st).

Continue straight in patt at armhole edge, and continue to dec 1 st at neck edge of every fourth row until 19/20/21/22 sts rem.****

Continue straight in patt until armhole corresponds in length with back, with right side facing for next row.

Shape shoulder

Keeping continuity of patt, bind off 6/6/7/7 sts, patt to end of row. Patt 1 row straight. Rep these 2 rows once more. Bind off the rem 7/8/7/8 sts.

Right front

With right side facing, rejoin yarn and bind off the next (center front) st; keeping continuity, patt the rem 55/58/61/64 sts from spare needle. Dec 1 st at end (neck edge) of next and every foll fourth row. When front corresponds in length with back at beg of armhole shaping, and with wrong side facing for next row, **continue to dec at neck edge on every fourth row** and shape armhole as for left front from *** to ****.

Continue straight in patt until armhole corresponds in length with back, with wrong side facing for next row.
Shape shoulder as for left front.

FINISHING

Block back and front to measurements and press lightly on wrong side, omitting ribbing.
Sew back and front together at shoulders.

Armhole bands

With size 5(3¾mm) needles, cast on 9 sts and k1, p1 rib (right-side rows having a k1 at each end, and wrong-side rows having a p1 at each end) until band fits along armhole edge when very slightly stretched.
Sew bands to armholes.

Neckband

With size 5(3¾mm) needles, cast on 11 sts and k1, p1 rib as for armhole bands until band fits around neck edge when very slightly stretched.
Beg with cast-on end at center front, pin neckband along left front neck edge, across back neck, and down right front. Cross bound-off end over cast-on end and sew band in place.
Press seams very lightly on wrong side. Sew up side seams and press seams lightly on wrong side.

Rock and Sand Sweater

Hot days are rare in Lewis, but when they do happen, the beach at the village of Coll on Broad Bay is a particularly good sun trap, and the sand glows. **I** was attracted by a large rock protruding through the sand, and used both its color and shape to design the interesting yoke on this sweater. **T**he body has patterns of light and dark fawn, reflecting the ripples and shading of the surrounding sand. **T**he result is a casual sweater with a rugged, country look.

RATING ● ● ● ●

Rock and Sand Sweater

SIZES
To fit chest 38/40/42/44in(97/102/107/112cm)

KNITTED MEASUREMENTS
Chest 44/46/48/50in
(112/117/122/127cm)
Length from top of shoulder
25/25½/26/26½in(63.5/65/66/67.5cm)
Sleeve length 19½/20/20½/21in(49.5/51/52/53.5cm)

MATERIALS
Shetland 3-ply yarn, 170yds per 2oz(139m per 50g): 5/5/5/6 2oz(50g) hanks in light fawn; 4/4/5/5 2oz(50g) hanks in dark fawn; 1 2oz(50g) hank in old gold mix; 1 2oz(50g) hank in blue gold mix; 1 2oz(50g) hank in green gold mix.

1 pair each size 5(3¾mm) and size 7(4½mm) needles
Safety pin

GAUGE
23 sts and 23 rows to 4in(10.25cm) measured over chart A patt, using size 7(4½mm) needles.

BACK AND FRONT (2 PIECES ALIKE)
With size 5(3¾mm) needles and light fawn, cast on 102/106/110/116 sts. K1, p1 rib for 3in(8cm).

Next row—Increase
Rib 7/5/3/2, *m1, rib 4; rep from * to the last 7/5/3/2 sts; m1, rib 7/5/3/2—125/131/137/145 sts.

Change to size 7(4½mm) needles and, joining in dark fawn, work the patt from chart A as follows:
Patt the 4/7/10/0 edge sts; rep the first 14 patt sts 4/4/4/5 times; patt the 5 center sts; rep the next 14 patt sts 4/4/4/5 times; patt the 4/7/10/0 edge sts, as indicated on chart.

Continue in this manner, repeating the 14 patt rows 5 times. Then work the first 6 rows once more (76 patt rows total).

Divide for V shaping
Continue in patt (row7), and work 62/65/68/72 sts; place the next st (center front) on a safety pin; place the rem sts on a spare needle.

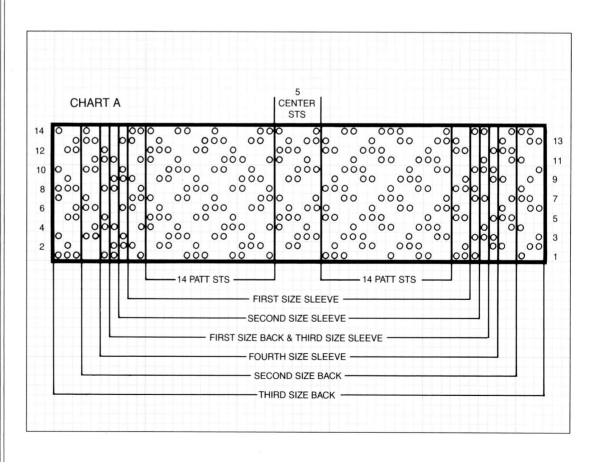

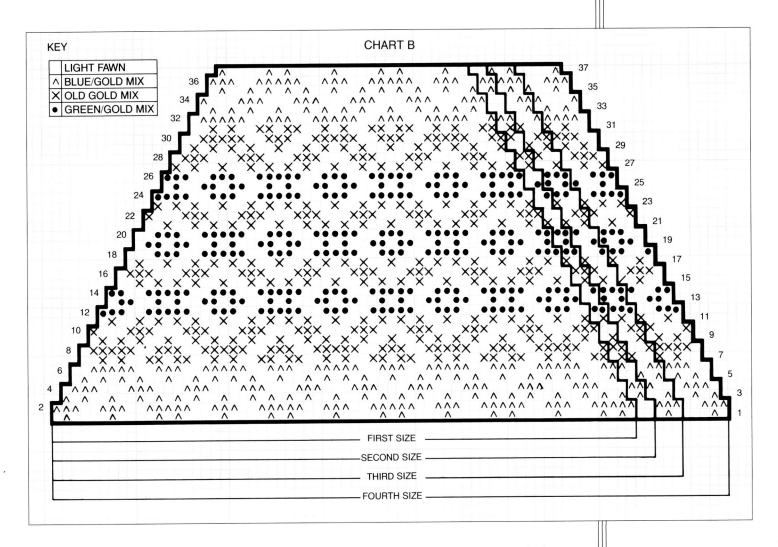

CHART B

KEY

	LIGHT FAWN
∧	BLUE/GOLD MIX
X	OLD GOLD MIX
•	GREEN/GOLD MIX

— FIRST SIZE —
— SECOND SIZE —
— THIRD SIZE —
— FOURTH SIZE —

Shape right side

Turn, and keeping continuity of patt, work these first 62/65/68/72 sts as follows:

Row 1: p2tog in light fawn, patt to end of row.

Row 2: patt to the last 2 sts, k2tog in light fawn.

Rep these 2 rows until 1 st remains. Break off dark fawn and, with light fawn, bind off last st.

Shape left side

With right side of work facing, rejoin yarns to the 62/65/68/72 sts on spare needle, and keeping continuity (row 7), patt to end of row. Shape as follows:

Row 1: patt to the last 2 sts, p2tog tbl in light fawn.

Row 2: ssk in light fawn, patt to end of row.

Rep these 2 rows until 1 st remains. Break off dark fawn and, with light fawn, bind off last st.

Yoke

With size 7(4½mm) needles, light fawn, and right side of work facing, knit up 70/72/75/80 sts along decreased edge of right side, from single bound-off st to center front safety pin; pick up and k the st from safety pin; knit up 70/72/75/80 sts along decreased edge of left side, to single bound-off st—141/145/151/161 sts.

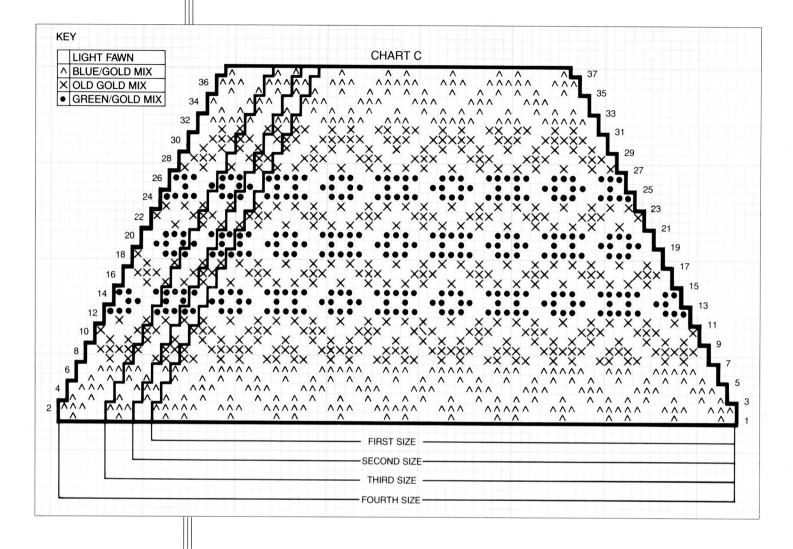

KEY

	LIGHT FAWN
^	BLUE/GOLD MIX
X	OLD GOLD MIX
•	GREEN/GOLD MIX

CHART C

FIRST SIZE

SECOND SIZE

THIRD SIZE

FOURTH SIZE

Work purl border as follows:
Row 1 (wrong side): k70/72/75/80, p1, k70/72/75/80.
Row 2: ssk, p67/69/72/77, sl2tog knitwise, k1, p2sso, p67/69/72/77, k2tog.
Row 3: k68/70/73/78, p1, k68/70/73/78.

Patt yoke as follows:
Next row: ssk, k65/67/70/75, sl2tog knitwise, k1, p2sso, k65/67/70/75, k2tog.
Next row: purl.

Joining in and breaking off colors as required, shape yoke and work patt from charts B and C as follows:
Row 1 (right side): with light fawn ssk, work row 1 of patt from chart B over the next 63/65/68/73 sts, with light fawn sl2tog knitwise, k1, p2sso, work row 1 of patt from chart C over the next 63/65/68/73 sts, with light fawn k2tog.

Row 2: with light fawn p1, work row 2 of patt from chart C over the next 63/65/68/73 sts, with light fawn p1, work row 2 of chart B over the next 63/65/68/73 sts, with light fawn p1.

Continue in this manner, with light fawn, working an ssk at beg, a double dec at center, and a k2tog at end, on every right-side row, and work patts from charts on rem sts as indicated. On wrong-side rows, work decreased sts in light fawn. Work all 37 rows of charts—57/61/67/77 sts rem. Break off all colors except light fawn, and purl 1 row.

Next row: with light fawn, knit, double decreasing at center of row as set—55/59/65/75 sts rem.

Third and fourth sizes only

Rep these last 2 rows 1/3 times more—63/69 sts rem.

All sizes

Next row: k27/29/31/34, p1, k27/29/31/34. Work purl border as follows:
Row 1 (right side): m1, p26/28/30/33, sl2tog knitwise, k1, p2sso, p25/27/29/32, m1, p1.
Row 2: k27/29/31/34, p1, k27/29/31/34.
Row 3: As row 1—55/59/63/69 sts.

Working in repeated stripes of 2 rows light fawn / 2 rows blue gold / 2 rows light fawn / 2 rows old gold / 2 rows light fawn / 2 rows green gold, work neck as follows:
Row 1 (wrong side): (p1, k1) 13/14/15/17 times; (first, second, and third sizes only—p next st); all sizes—p center st; (first, second, and third sizes only—p next st); all sizes—(k1, p1) 13/14/15/17 times.
Row 2: k1, m1, then rib as set to center 3 sts; sl2tog knitwise, k1, p2sso, rib as set to the last st, m1, k1.

Continue in this manner, increasing 1 st at beg and end, and decreasing 2 sts at center of every right-side row, and working all increased sts into rib patt, and k the first and last sts on right-side rows, and p these sts on wrong side rows.

Work until neck measures 3in(8cm) when measured from beg of inc, with wrong side facing for next row. Then continue in stripes and rib as set, but working increases and decreases on next and every foll wrong-side row for a further 3in(8cm). Break off all colors except light fawn, and bind off in rib.

SLEEVES

With size 5(3¾mm) needles and light fawn, cast on 54/54/56/58 sts. K1, p1 rib for 3in(8cm).

Next row—Increase

Rib 5/1/2/3, *m1, rib 4; rep from * to the last 5/1/2/3 sts; rib 5/1/2/3—65/67/69/71 sts.

Change to size 7(4½mm) needles, join in dark fawn, and work the patt from chart A as follows:
Patt the 2/3/4/5 edge sts; rep the first 14 patt sts twice; patt 5 center sts; rep the next 14 patt sts twice; patt the 2/3/4/5 edge sts, as indicated on chart.

Continue in this manner, and inc 1 st at each end of every third row, until there are 93/97/93/89 sts. Patt 3 rows straight, then inc 1 st at each end of next and every foll fourth row, until there are 119/123/125/127 sts. Work all increased sts into patt. Continue straight in patt until sleeve measures 19½/20/20½/21in(49.5/51/52/53.5cm) from beg, with right side facing for next row. Break off dark fawn and, with light fawn, bind off all sts.

FINISHING

Press all pieces lightly on wrong side, omitting ribbings. Sew back and front together at shoulder seams, sewing the last 3in(8cm) of neck on right side. Place center top of sleeves at shoulder seams, and sew sleeves to body. Press seams lightly on wrong side. Sew up side and sleeve seams. Press seams lightly on wrong side, omitting ribbings.

Sand Stitch Cotton Sweater

A *walk along the beach below the village of Gress revealed the usual seaborne debris, including a length of well-bleached rope lying in the sand.* **A** *plaited cable, modeled after the rope, appears on the trim of this simple, elegant sweater and contrasts with the texture of the grainy sand stitch.*

RATING ● ●

Sand Stitch Cotton Sweater

SIZES
To fit chest
38/40/42/44in(97/102/107/112cm)

KNITTED MEASUREMENTS
Chest 43/45/47/49in(110/115/119/125cm)
Length from top of shoulder
27/27½/28/28½in(69/70/71/72.5cm)
Sleeve length
19/19½/20/20½in(48.5/49.5/51/52cm)

MATERIALS
17/18/18/19 1¾oz(50g) balls of mercerized cotton, 95 yds per 1¾oz(88m per 50g)
1 pair each size 4(3½mm) and size 7(4½mm) needles
1 cable needle

GAUGE
11 sts and 13 rows to 2in(5cm) measured over sand stitch patt, using size 7(4½mm) needles.

BACK AND FRONT (2 ALIKE)
With size 4(3½mm) needles, cast on 101/105/109/113 sts. Work rib as follows:
Row 1: *k1, p1; rep from * to the last st; k1.
Row 2: *p1, k1; rep from * to the last st; p1.

Rep these 2 rows until rib measures 2¾in(7cm).

Next row—Increase
Rib 8/5/7/4, *m1, rib 5; rep from * to the last 8/5/7/4 sts; m1, rib 8/5/7/4—119/125/129/135 sts.

Change to size 7(4½mm) needles and work sand stitch patt as follows:
Row 1 (right side): knit.
Row 2: knit.
Row 3: *k1, p1; rep from * to the last st; k1.
Row 4: *p1, k1; rep from * to the last st; p1.

Rep these 4 rows until back measures 16¾/17/17¼/17½in(42.5/43.5/44/44.5cm) from beg, with right side facing for next row.

Shape armholes
Keeping continuity of patt, bind off 10 sts at beg of next 2 rows—99/105/109/115 sts. Then continue straight in patt until armhole measures 7½/7¾/8/8¼in(19/20/20.5/21cm), with right side facing for next row.

Shape neck and shoulders
Patt 40/42/43/45 sts; place the rem sts on a spare needle. Keeping continuity of patt, work shoulder as follows:
Row 1: sl the first st and bind it off; then bind off the next 3 sts; patt to end of row.
Row 2: patt to the last 2 sts; k2tog.
Row 3: sl the first st and bind it off; then bind off the next 2 sts; patt to end of row.
Row 4: as row 2.
Row 5: as row 3.
Row 6: as row 2.

Bind off the rem 27/29/30/32 sts.

With right side facing, rejoin yarn and bind off the next (center) 19/21/23/25 sts from spare needle; patt the rem 40/42/43/45 sts. Keeping continuity of patt, shape shoulder as follows:
Next row: patt to the last 2 sts; k2tog.
Now work rows 1 through 5 of first shoulder. Bind off the rem 27/29/30/32 sts.

SLEEVES
With size 4(3½mm) needles, cast on 51/53/53/55 sts. Rib as back and front for 2¾in(7cm).

Next row—Increase
Rib 1/2/4/0, *m1, rib 7/7/5/6; rep from * to the last 1/2/4/1 sts; m1, rib 1/2/4/1—59/61/63/65 sts.

Change to size 7(4½mm) needles and work in sand stitch patt as for back and front, and inc 1 st at each end of third and every foll third row until there are 71/71/79/79 sts. Patt 3 rows straight, then inc 1 st at each end of next and every foll fourth row until there are 113/115/119/121 sts. Work all increased sts into sand stitch patt.

Continue straight in patt until sleeve measures 19/19½/20/20½in(48.5/49.5/51/52cm) from beg. Mark center stitch of row. Bind off all sts.

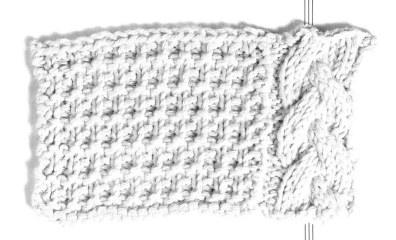

Cabled Neck/Shoulder Bands (2 alike)
With size 7(4½mm) needles, cast on 13 sts. Patt as follows:
Row 1 (right side): sl1, p1, k9, p1, k1.
Row 2: sl1, k1, p9, k2.
Row 3: sl1, p1, sl next 3 sts to cn and hold at front, k3, then k3 from cn, k3, p1, k1.
Row 4: as row 2.
Row 5: as row 1.
Row 6: as row 2.
Row 7: sl1, p1, k3, sl next 3 sts to cn and hold at back, k3, then k3 from cn, p1, k1.
Row 8: as row 2.

Rep these 8 rows until band fits across top of piece, from beg of first shoulder along neckline, to end of second shoulder.

FINISHING
Sew back neck/shoulder band to back, beg with cast-on end of band at right shoulder. Sew front band to front, beg with cast-on end of band at left shoulder. Sew back and front bands together at shoulders.

Cabled armhole bands (2 alike)
With size 7(4½mm) needles, cast on 13 sts and work cable patt as for neck/shoulder bands, until armhole bands fit along armhole from back armhole bind-off to front armhole bind-off.

Sew armhole bands along armholes, sewing cast-on end of band to back armhole bind-off, and sewing bound-off end of band to front armhole bind-off.

Place center top of sleeves (marked st) at center of armhole bands and sew sleeves to armhole bands. Press seams lightly on wrong side, omitting ribs.

Sew up side and sleeve seams, and press seams lightly on wrong side, omitting ribs.

Geodh' a' Chuibhrig

Check Rock Sweater

Geodh'a' Chuibhrig deserves a special word because it is a very special place—a secluded shingle bay surrounded by high cliffs, accessible only by a careful scramble. The rock of the cliffs has varied colors that seem to change according to light and wetness, creating the effect of a subtle patchwork quilt. Indeed, this effect inspired the Gaelic name Geodh'a' Chuibhrig, or "Quilt Cove." Just a single rock has been used as the source for this all-occasion sweater in a silk/wool mix. The typically colorful rock is reflected in lightly textured checks, with Swiss darning. The sweater has dropped shoulders and a simple shape.

RATING ● ● ● ●

Check Rock Sweater

SIZES
To fit chest 38–40in(97–102cm)

KNITTED MEASUREMENTS
Chest 45in(114cm)
Length from top of shoulder 26in(66cm)
Sleeve length 20½in(52cm)

MATERIALS
Silk/wool yarn, 132yds per 1¾oz(121m per 50g):
7 1¾oz(50g) hanks in dark green; 6 1¾oz(50g) hanks in blue; 2 1¾oz(50g) hanks in beige; 1¾oz(50g) hank each of purple, dark blue, dusky pink, and pale turquoise.
1 pair each size 4(3½mm) and size 6(4mm) needles
Stitch holders
7 jacquard bobbins

GAUGE
11 sts and 14 rows to 2in(5cm) measured over st st, using size 6(4mm) needles.

BACK
With size 4(3½mm) needles and dark green, cast on 112 sts. K1, p1 rib in colors as follows:
2 rows dark green / 2 rows purple / 2 rows blue / 2 rows beige. Rep these 8 rows until rib measures 3in(8cm).

Next row—Increase
With beige, rib 3, *m1, rib 5; rep from * to the last 4 sts; m1, rib 4—134 sts.

Fill 7 jacquard bobbins with dark green yarn (for instructions on how to make bobbins, see page xiii).

Change to size 6(4mm) needles and, joining in and breaking off colors as required, patt as follows:
Row 1: with dark green, knit.
Row 2: with dark green, purl.
Row 3: *join in dark green bobbin and (k2 dark green, k1 blue) twice, k2 dark green, then cross dark green yarn over blue yarn before working next st to avoid gap, and k13 blue; rep from * (using a new bobbin each time) to the last 8 sts; join in dark green bobbin and (k2 dark green, k1 blue) twice, k2 dark green.
Row 4: using single ball of dark green, *p1 dark green, p1 dusky pink; rep from * to end of row.
Row 5: with same ball of dark green, * k1 dark green, k1 purple; rep from * to end of row.
Row 6: *pick up dark green bobbin from directly below and (p2 dark green, p1 blue) twice, p2 dark green, then cross dark green yarn over blue yarn before working next st to avoid gap, and p13 blue; rep from * to the last 8 sts; pick up dark green bobbin from directly below and (p2 dark green, p1 blue) twice, p2 dark green.
Row 7: as row 1.
Row 8: as row 2.
Row 9: as row 3, using bobbins as set.
Row 10: as row 6.
Row 11: *with dark blue, sl8 purlwise with yarn at back, (k1, sl1 purlwise with yarn at back) 6 times, k1; rep from * to the last 8 sts; sl8 purlwise with yarn at back.
Row 12: *with dark blue, sl8 purlwise with yarn at front, (k1, sl1 purlwise with yarn at front) 6 times, k1; rep from * to the last 8 sts; sl8 purlwise with yarn at front.
Row 13: as row 3, using bobbins as set.
Row 14: as row 6.

Row 15: with beige, as row 11.
Row 16: with beige, as row 12.
Row 17: as row 3, using bobbins as set.
Row 18: as row 6.
Row 19: with pale turquoise, as row 11.
Row 20: with pale turquoise, as row 12.
Row 21: as row 3, using bobbins as set.
Row 22: as row 6.
Row 23: as row 15.
Row 24: as row 16.
Row 25: as row 3, using bobbins as set.
Row 26: as row 6.
Row 27: as row 11.
Row 28: as row 12.
Row 29: as row 3, using bobbins as set.
Row 30: as row 6.

Rep rows 1 through 30 until back measures 25in(64cm) from beg, with right side facing for next row.

Shape neck and shoulders
Patt 47 sts; place the next 40 sts on a holder for back neck; place the rem sts on a spare needle.

Keeping continuity of patt, work the 47 sts of right shoulder, decreasing 1 st at neck edge of next and every foll alt row until 42 sts rem. Bind off shoulder sts.

With right side facing, rejoin appropriate yarns to the 47 sts of left shoulder and, keeping continuity of patt, work 1 row. Then dec at neck edge of next and every foll alt row until 42 sts rem. Bind off shoulder sts.

FRONT
Work as for back until front measures 23in(58.5cm) from beg, with right side facing for next row.

Shape neck and shoulders
Patt 52 sts; place the next 30 sts on a holder for front neck; place the rem sts on a spare needle.

Keeping continuity of patt, work the 52 sts of left shoulder, decreasing 1 st at neck edge of next and every foll alt row until 42 sts rem. Then continue straight in patt until front corresponds in length with back at shoulder. Bind off shoulder sts.

With right side facing, rejoin appropriate yarns to the 52 sts of right shoulder and, keeping continuity of patt, work 1 row. Then dec 1 st at neck edge of next and every foll alt row until 42 sts rem. Continue straight in patt until front corresponds in length with back at shoulder. Bind off shoulder sts.

SLEEVES
With size 4(3½mm) needles and dark green, cast on 54 sts. K1, p1 rib in color sequence as for back for 3in(8cm).

Next row—Increase
With beige, rib 6, *m1, rib 3; rep from * to the last 6 sts; m1, rib 6—69 sts.

Change to size 6(4mm) needles and, with dark green, work in st st for 2 rows.
Next row (right side): with blue, knit, increasing 1 st at each end of row—71 sts.
Next row: with dark green, purl.

Joining in and breaking off colors as required, patt as for back, beg at row 1 and repeating the 30 patt rows. **At the same time,** shape sleeve as follows:

Check Rock Sweater

check Stitch sweater in 7 colors.
silk/wool mix yarn
Textured checks with Swiss darned stripes

crew neck.
All ribbings striped

dropped shoulder

*Inc 1 st at each end of every fourth row twice; then inc 1 st at each end of every foll seventh row 3 times; patt 1 row straight; rep from * until there are 123 sts in total, and keeping continuity, work all increased sts into patt.

Continue until 5 complete patt repeats have been worked, and then work rows 1 through 5 once again. With dark green, bind off all sts.

FINISHING

On back, front, and sleeves, Swiss darn (see page xiii) the central 2-st vertical dark green stripes, as shown in photograph, darning every second st vertically on the right of stripe in purple, working from top to bottom, and every alt second st vertically on the left in dusky pink, working from top to bottom.

Press pieces very lightly on wrong side, omitting ribbing. Sew back and front together at left shoulder.

Neckband

With right side facing, size 4(3½mm) needles, and dark green, knit up 8 sts to back neck holder; pick up and knit the 40 sts from back neck holder; knit up 8 sts to shoulder seam; knit up 17 sts to front neck holder; pick up and knit the 30 sts from front neck holder; knit up 17 sts to shoulder bind-off—120 sts.

K1, p1 rib in color sequence as for back for 3in(8cm). Bind off loosely and evenly in rib.

Sew up right shoulder and neckband seam. Turn neckband in half to the inside and slip st in position. Press shoulder seams lightly on wrong side.

Place center top of sleeves at shoulder seams and sew sleeves to body. Press seams lightly on wrong side.

Sew up side and sleeve seams. Press seams lightly on wrong side.

Textured Multicolor Sweater

At one end of the cove there is a sea cave, cut deep into the cliff. Inside this cathedral atmosphere, sheets of almost tangible light bounce off the sea and play upon the wet cave walls, carved over time into fantastic shapes. Watching the interplay of light, color, and texture is rather like watching the flickering of a fire, and I have never seen the same effect twice. To capture just one of the cave's moods, I used yarn hand-dyed in random colors, although mauve is predominant. The result is a sweater both rich and exotic.

RATING ●●●●

Textured Multicolor Sweater

SIZES
To fit chest
38/40/42/44in(97/102/107/112cm)

KNITTED MEASUREMENTS
Chest
44/46½/48¾/51in(112/118/124/130cm)
Length from top of shoulder
26½/27/27½/28in(67.5/68.5/70/71cm)
Sleeve length
20½/20½/21/21in(52/52/53.5/53.5cm)

MATERIALS
3/4/4/4 3½oz(100g) hanks of sportweight
wool in solid color
5 3½oz(100g) hanks of sportweight wool
in multicolor
1 pair each size 5(3¾mm), size 7(4½mm),
and size 8(5mm) needles
2 sfitch holders
Stitch markers

GAUGE
12 sts and 20 rows to 2in(5cm) measured
over main patt, using size 8(5mm) needles.
To work a gauge swatch, cast on 30 sts and
patt as for back for 28 rows.

BACK
**With size 5(3¾mm) needles and mauve,
cast on 112/120/126/132 sts. K1, p1 rib,
working 2 rows mauve / 2 rows multi, repeated for 3in(8cm).

Next row—Increase
Rib 3/7/5/3, *m1, rib 5; rep from * to the
last 4/8/6/4 sts; m1, rib 4/8/6/4—
134/142/150/158 sts.

Change to size 8(5mm) needles and work
main patt as follows:
Row 1 (right side): with mauve, knit.
Row 2: with mauve, k6, *sl2 purlwise with
yarn at front, k6; rep from * to end of row.
Row 3: with mauve, k6, *sl2 purlwise with
yarn at back, k6; rep from * to end of row.
Row 4: as row 2.
Rows 5 & 7: with multi, k6, *sl2 purlwise
with yarn at back, k6; rep from * to end of
row.
Rows 6 & 8: with multi, p6, *sl2 purlwise
with yarn at front; p6; rep from * to end of
row.
Row 9: with mauve, as row 1.
Row 10: with mauve, k2, *sl2 purlwise
with yarn at front, k6; rep from * to the last
4 sts; sl2 purlwise with yarn at front, k2.
Row 11: with mauve, k2, *sl2 purlwise
with yarn at back, k6; rep from * to the last
4 sts; sl2 purlwise with yarn at back, k2.
Row 12: as row 10.
Rows 13 & 15: with multi, k2, *sl2 purlwise with yarn at back, k6; rep from * to the
last 4 sts; sl2 purlwise with yarn at back, k2.
Rows 14 & 16: with multi, p2, *sl2 purlwise with yarn at front, k6; rep from * to
the last 4 sts; sl2 purlwise with yarn at
front, k2.

Rep rows 1 through 16. When back measures 16/16¼/16½/16¾in(41/41.5/42/
42.5cm) from beg, place a marker at each
end of row to mark beg of armholes. Then
continue to work in main patt until the 16
patt rows have been worked 11 times in total. Then work the first 4/4/12/12 rows
once more (180/180/188/188 patt rows in
total). Back should now measure 21/21/
21¾/21¾in(53.5/53.5/55.5/55.5cm) from
beg, with right side facing for next row.
Dec 8 sts evenly across last row of patt.
Break off mauve—126/134/142/150 sts.

Change to size 7(4½mm) needles, and with multi work pearl rib as follows:
Row 1 (right side): *k1, p1; rep from * to end of row.
Row 2: *k1 into row below, p1; rep from * to end of row.***

Rep these 2 rows until back measures 26½/27/27½/28in(67.5/68.5/70/71cm) from beg, with right side facing for next row.

Shape shoulders
Keeping continuity of patt, bind off 10/10/11/12 sts at beg of next 2 rows. Bind off 10/11/11/12 sts at beg of next 2 rows. Bind off 10/11/12/12 sts at beg of next 4 rows. Place the rem 46/48/50/54 sts on a holder for back neck.

FRONT
Work as for back from ** to ***

Rep the 2 pearl rib rows until armholes measure 8¼/8½/8½/8¾in(21/21.5/21.5/22cm), with right side facing for next row.

Shape neck
Patt the first 48/51/54/56 sts; place the next 30/32/34/38 sts on a holder for front neck; place the rem sts on a spare needle.

Turn, and keeping continuity, patt the first 48/51/54/56 sts, decreasing 1 st at neck edge of next and every foll alt row until 40/43/46/48 sts rem. When armhole corresponds in length with that of back, and with right side facing for next row, shape shoulder as follows:

†Bind off 10/10/11/12 sts, patt to end of row.
Patt 1 row straight. Bind off 10/11/11/12 sts, patt to end of row.
Patt 1 row straight. Bind off 10/11/12/12 sts, patt to end of row.
Rep the last 2 rows once more.††

With right side facing, rejoin yarn and, keeping continuity, patt the 48/51/54/56 sts from spare needle. Turn, and keeping continuity, dec 1 st at neck edge of next and every foll alt row until 40/43/46/48 sts rem. When armhole corresponds in length with that of back, and with wrong side facing for next row, shape shoulder as given for previous side, from † to ††.

SLEEVES
With size 5(3¾mm) needles and mauve, cast on 60/60/64/64 sts. K1, p1 rib in stripes as back for 3in(8cm).

Next row—Increase
Rib 3/3/6/6, *m1, rib 6/6/4/4; rep from * to the last 3/3/6/6 sts; m1, rib 3/3/6/6—70/70/78/78 sts.

Change to size 8(5mm) needles and work main patt as for back, increasing 1 st at each end of second/second/eighth/eighth row. Then inc 1 st at each end of every foll sixth row until there are 126/128/134/138 sts. Work all increased sts into patt. **Note:** Do not begin or end a row with sl sts. Instead, work these sts plain (garter st for mauve, st st for multi) until 1 st can be worked before the sl sts at the beg of a row, and after the sl sts at the end of a row.

If necessary, continue straight in patt, ending after 4 mauve rows, when sleeve measures approx 20½/20½/21/21in (52/52/53.5/53.5cm) from beg, with right side facing for next row. Bind off all sts.

FINISHING
Do not press garment pieces. Sew back and front together at left shoulder seam.

Textured
Multicolor
Sweater

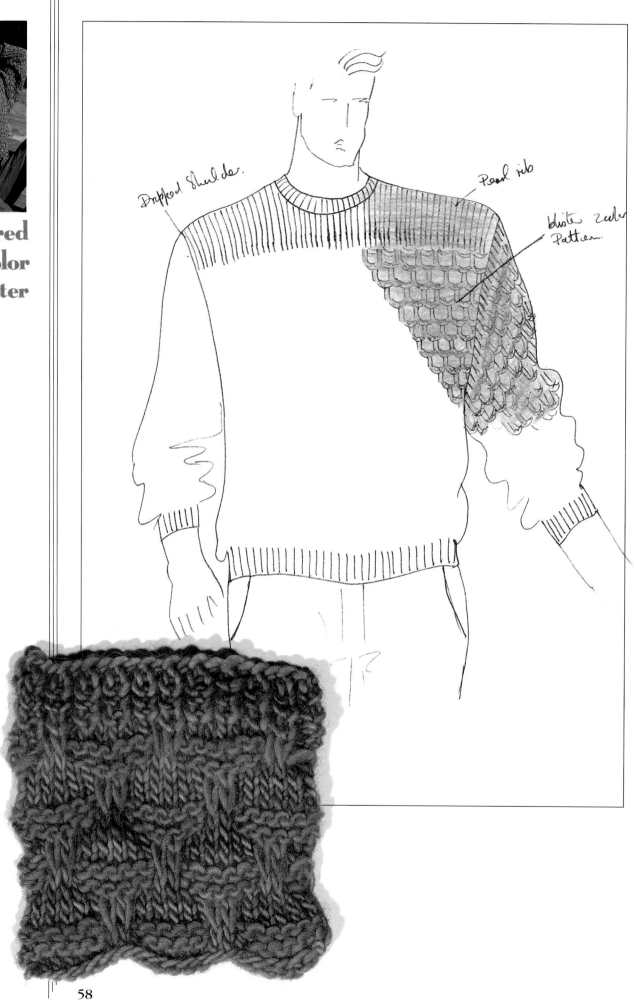

Dropped shoulder.

Pearl rib

kluster Zader
Pattern

Neckband

With right side facing, size 5(3¾mm) needles, and multi, pick up and knit the 46/48/50/54 sts from back neck holder; knit up 17/17/18/18 sts to front neck holder; pick up and knit the 30/32/34/38 sts from front neck holder; knit up 17/17/18/18 sts to top of shoulder—110/114/120/128 sts. K1, p1 rib for 3½in(9cm). Bind off all sts loosely and evenly.

Sew up right shoulder and neckband seam. Turn neckband in half to the inside and slip stitch in position.

Place center top of sleeves at shoulder seams and sew sleeves to body between markers. Press armhole seams very lightly on the wrong side.

Sew up side and sleeve seams. Press seams very lightly on the wrong side, omitting ribs.

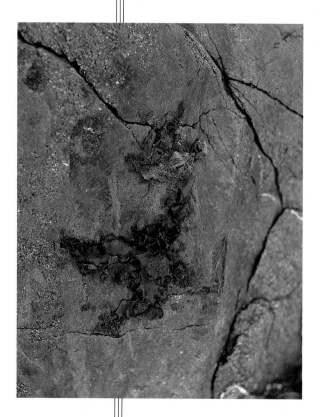

Mohair Sweater

A piece of wine-colored seaweed on blue gneiss offers one of nature's most unusual color combinations—simple yet striking. **T**he colors are combined here in an elegant and geometric Fair Isle pattern, while the use of mohair yarn helps to capture their richness and luster.

RATING ● ●

Mohair Sweater

SIZES

To fit chest
38/40/42/44in(97/102/107/112cm)

KNITTED MEASUREMENTS

Chest 44/46/48/50in(112/117/122/127cm)
Length from top of shoulder
26½/27/27½/28in(67.5/68.5/70/71cm)
Sleeve length
19½/20/20/20½in(49.5/51/51/52cm)

MATERIALS

Standard mohair yarn, 76 yds per oz(125m
per 50g):
13/13/14/14 1oz(25g) balls in claret;
4/5/5/5 1oz(25g) balls in midnight blue;
4/4/5/5 1oz(25g) balls in dark navy.

1 pair each size 7(4½mm) and size
9(5½mm) needles
2 stitch holders
Stitch markers

GAUGE

19 sts and 18 rows to 4in(10cm) measured
over patt, using size 9(5½mm) needles.

BACK

**With size 7(4½mm) needles and claret,
cast on 92/96/100/102 sts. K1, p1 rib for
3in(8cm).

Next row—Increase

Rib 4/6/1/3, *m1, rib 7/6/7/6; rep from * to
the last 4/6/1/3 sts; m1, rib 4/6/1/3—
105/111/115/119 sts.

Change to size 9(5½mm) needles, and
joining in and breaking off colors as required, work the patt from chart, repeating
the 18 patt sts 5/6/6/6 times, and working
the first 7/1/3/5 sts and the last 8/2/4/6 sts
on right-side rows, and the first 8/2/4/6 sts
and the last 7/1/6/3 sts on wrong-side rows,
as indicated on chart.

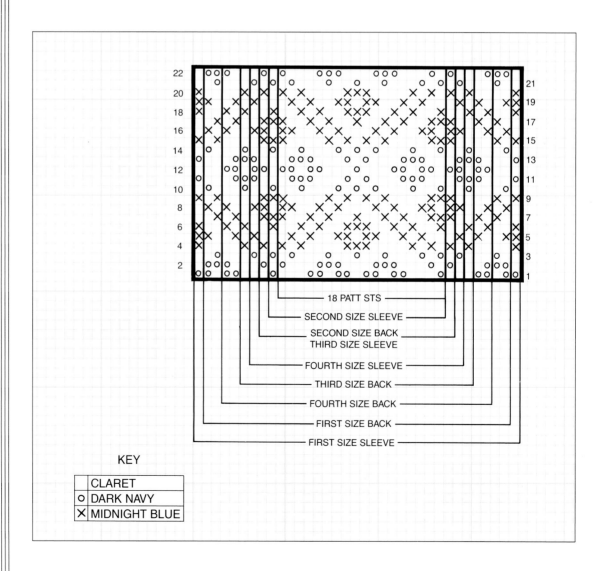

KEY

	CLARET
o	DARK NAVY
X	MIDNIGHT BLUE

Continue as set, repeating the 22 patt rows until back measures 16/16/16¼/16½in (41/41/41.5/42cm) from beg. Place a marker at each end of row to mark beg of armholes.***

Continue as set until armholes measure 10½//11/11¼/11½in(27/28/28.5/29cm).

Shape shoulders

Keeping continuity of patt, bind off 11/12/12/13 sts at beg of next 2 rows. Bind off 12/12/13/13 sts at beg of next 2 rows. Bind off 12/13/13/13 sts at beg of foll 2 rows. Place the rem 35/37/39/41 sts on a holder for back neck.

FRONT

Work as for back from ** to ***.

Continue as set until armholes measure 8½/9/9¼/9½in(21.5/23/23.5/24cm), with right side facing for next row.

Shape neck

Patt 41/43/44/45 sts; place the next 23/25/27/29 sts on a holder for front neck; place the rem 41/43/44/45 sts on a spare needle.

†††Turn, and keeping continuity of patt, dec 1 st at neck edge of the next 3 rows. Patt 1 row straight. Dec 1 st at neck edge of next and every foll alt row until 35/37/38/39 sts rem.††††

Shape left shoulder

Next row (right side): bind off 11/12/12/13, patt to end of row. Patt 1 row straight.
Next row: bind off 12/12/13/13, patt to end of row. Patt 1 row straight. Bind off the rem 12/13/13/13 sts.

With right side facing, rejoin yarns to the sts on spare needle and, keeping continuity, patt to end of row. Then work as previous side, from ††† to ††††. Patt 1 row.

Shape right shoulder

Next row (wrong side): bind off 11/12/12/13 sts, patt to end of row. Patt 1 row straight.
Next row: bind off 12/12/13/13, patt to end of row. Patt 1 row straight. Bind off the rem 12/13/13/13 sts.

SLEEVES

With size 7(4½mm) needles and claret, cast on 44/46/48/50 sts. K1, p1 rib for 2¾in(7cm).

Next row—Increase

Rib 2/3/4/1, *m1, rib 5/5/5/6; rep from* to the last 2/3/4/1 sts; m1, rib 2/3/4/1—53/55/57/59 sts.

Change to size 9(5½mm) needles, and joining in and breaking off colors as required, work the patt from chart, repeating the 18 patt sts 2/3/3/3 times, and working the first 8/0/1/2 sts and the last 9/1/2/3 sts on right-side rows, and the first 9/1/2/3 sts and the last 8/0/1/2 sts on wrong-side rows, as indicated on chart.

Continue as set, and inc 1 st at each end of every third row until there are 101/105/107/109 sts. Work all increased sts into patt. Then continue straight in patt until sleeve measures 19½/20/20/20½in(49.5/51/51/52cm) from beg. Bind off all sts.

**Mohair
Sweater**

Two Color Mohair Sweater
Classic style - Round neck/set in sleeve
Fair Isle pattern.

Sizes. 38/40/42/44 in

FINISHING

Sew back and front together at left shoulder seam.

Neckband

With right side facing, size 7(4½mm) needles, and claret, pick up and knit the 35/37/39/41 sts from back neck holder; knit up 11 sts to front neck holder; pick up and knit the 23/25/27/29 sts from front neck holder; knit up 11 sts to top of right shoulder—80/84/88/92 sts.

K1, p1 rib for 10 rows. Bind off loosely and evenly.

Sew up right shoulder and neckband seam.

Place center top of sleeves at shoulder seams and sew sleeves to body between markers. Omitting neckband rib, press seams very lightly on wrong side.

Sew up side and sleeve seams. Press seams very lightly on wrong side, omitting rib.

Check Stitch Sweater

In the middle of Geodh'a' Chuibhrig, there is a massive black rock, wave smoothed and about twenty feet high, where it is possible to lie and watch the tide coming in over the surrounding shingle. The shifting water is hypnotically fascinating, and the feeling of motion and depth inspired this rugged, outdoor sweater with a deeply textured pattern.

RATING ● ●

Check Stitch Sweater

SIZES
To fit chest 38–40/42–44in(97–102/107–112cm)

KNITTED MEASUREMENTS
Chest 46¾/51in(119/130cm)
Length from top of shoulder 26/26¾in(66/68cm)
Sleeve length 20/20½in(51/52cm)

MATERIALS
8/9 4 oz(112g) hanks of heavyweight yarn, 200yds per 4 oz(163m per 100g)
1 pair each size 6(4mm) and size 8 (5mm) needles
Stitch holders
2 buttons

GAUGE
9 sts and 12 rows to 2in(5cm) measured over gauge patt, using size 8(5mm) needles. Work a gauge swatch as follows: with size 8(5mm) needles, cast on 20 sts.
Rows 1 & 2: *k2, p2; rep from * to end.
Rows 3 & 4: *p2, k2; rep from * to end.
Work 20 rows total. Bind off all sts.

BACK
With size 6(4mm) needles, cast on 96/104 sts. K1, p1 rib for 2¾in(7cm)

Next row—Increase
Rib 2/7, *m1, rib 7/6; rep from * to the last 3/7 sts; m1, rib 3/7—110/120 sts.

Change to size 8(5mm) needles and patt as follows:

First size only
Rows 1, 5 & 9 (right side): *k2, p2; rep from * to the last 2 sts; k2.
Row 2 & all foll wrong-side rows: k the k sts and p the p sts as they present themselves.
Rows 3 & 7: (k2, p2) twice, *k4, p2, k2, p2; rep from * to the last 12 sts, k4, (p2, k2) twice.
Rows 11, 15 & 19: *p2, k2; rep from * to the last 2 sts, p2.
Rows 13 & 17: as rows 3 & 7.
Row 20: as row 2.

Second size only
Rows 1, 5 & 9 (right side): *k2, p2; rep from * to end of row.
Row 2 & all foll wrong-side rows: k the k sts and p the p sts as they present themselves.
Rows 3 & 7: (k2, p2) twice, *k4, p2, k2, p2; rep from * to the last 2 sts; k2.
Rows 11, 15 & 19: *p2, k2; rep from * to end of row.
Rows 13 & 17: as rows 3 & 7.
Row 20: as row 2.

All sizes
Rep the 20 patt rows until back measures 25/25¾in(64/65.5cm) from beg, with right side facing for next row.

Shape neck
Patt 41/44 sts; patt the next 28/32 sts and place these sts on a holder for back neck; patt the rem 41/44 sts. Keeping continuity of patt, work the last 41/44 sts, decreasing 1 st at neck edge of next and every foll alt row until 38/41 sts remain. Bind off these 38/41 sts. With wrong side facing, rejoin yarn to the first 41/44 sts and dec at neck edge as previously until 38/41 sts remain. Bind off all sts.

FRONT
Work as for back until front measures 18½/19in(47/48cm), ending with right side facing for next row.

Front neck opening

Patt 51/56 sts; then (k1, p1) 4 times; place the rem sts on a spare needle. Now work these 59/64 sts in k1, p1 rib over the inside 8 sts, and patt over 51/56 sts as set. Make a buttonhole on fourth and fifth sts of rib when front measures 20/20½in(51/52cm), and another at 22½/23¼in(57/59cm) from beg. (**To make buttonhole:** bind off 2 sts, then cast on 2 sts at same position on foll row.) Then continue straight as set until front measures 23¼/24in(59/61cm) from beg, with wrong side facing for next row.

Shape neck

Bind off 8 sts; patt as set to end of row.
Next row: patt to the last 3 sts and place these 3 sts on a holder.

Turn and patt 1 row straight.

Rep these last 2 rows once more, placing the 3 sts on same holder.
Next row: patt to the last 2 sts and place these 2 sts on same holder.

Turn and patt 1 row straight.

Rep these 2 rows once/twice more.

Now continue in patt, decreasing 1 st at beg (neck edge) of next and every foll alt row until 38/41 sts remain. If necessary, continue straight in patt until front corresponds in length with back at shoulder bind-off. Bind off all sts.

With size 8(5mm) needles, cast on 8 sts, then with right side of front facing, and keeping continuity of patt, pick up and patt the rem 51/56 sts from spare needle. Working the 8 cast-on sts in k1, p1 rib and the rem sts in patt as set, complete this side to correspond with previous one, but omitting buttonholes and reversing neck shaping.

SLEEVES

With size 6(4mm) needles, cast on 46 sts. K1, p1 rib for 3in(8cm).

Next row—Increase

Rib 3, *m1, rib 3; rep from * to the last 4 sts; m1, rib 4—60 sts.

Change to size 8(5mm) needles and work the patt as for second size, and inc 1 st at each end of eighth row, and thereafter every fourth row, until there are 100/106 sts. Work all increased sts into patt.

Continue straight in patt until sleeve measures 20/20½in(51/52cm) from beg. Bind off all sts.

FINISHING

Sew back and front at shoulder seams, and press seams lightly on wrong side.

Collar

With size 6(4mm) needles, and beg at right front neck, pick up and knit the first 3 sts from holder; knit up 1 st into neck edge; pick up and knit next 3 sts from holder; *knit up 1 st into neck edge; pick up and knit next 2 sts from holder; rep from * once/twice again; knit up 5 sts to shoulder seam; knit up 5 sts to back neck; pick up and knit the 28/32 sts from back neck holder; knit up 5 sts to shoulder seam; knit up 5 sts to left front holder; *pick up and knit next 2 sts from holder, knit up 1 st into neck edge; rep from * once/twice again; pick up and knit next 3 sts from holder; knit up 1 st into neck edge; pick up and knit last 3 sts from holder—74/84 sts total.

K1, p1 rib for 5in(13cm). Bind off loosely and evenly in rib.

Slip stitch lower end of right front rib in place.

Place center top of sleeves at shoulder seams and sew sleeves to body. Press seams lightly on wrong side.

Sew up side and sleeve seams. Press seams lightly on wrong side. Sew on buttons to correspond with buttonholes.

Moor and Mountain

Textured Chevron Sweater

Mist and moorland, and the outline of Beinn Mhor with its surrounding peaks. **S**oft, natural colors capture the effect, while chevrons convey the hill line in a sweater with a loose, casual style.

RATING ● ● ●

Textured Chevron Sweater

SIZES
To fit chest 40–42/44–46in(102–107/112–119cm)

KNITTED MEASUREMENTS
Chest 47½/52in(121/132cm)
Length from top of shoulder 27/28in(68.5/71cm)
Sleeve length 20/20½in(51/52cm)

MATERIALS
Sportweight yarn, 58yds per oz(95m per 50g):
9 1¾oz(50g) balls in natural; 7/8 1¾oz(50g) balls in gray; 6/7 1¾oz(50g) balls in charcoal.
1 pair each size 5(3¾mm), size 6(4mm), and size 7(4½mm) needles
Stitch markers

GAUGE
Work a gauge swatch as follows: with size 7(4½mm) needles, cast on 33 sts. Knit 1 row. Work chevron patt as for back for 20 rows. Bind off all sts.
When pinned flat without stretching, swatch should measure 4¾in(12cm) in width, and 3in(8cm) in length, measured along dec from point at cast-on edge to top.

BACK
**With size 5(3¾mm) needles and natural, cast on 130/138 sts. K1, p1 rib for 3in(8cm).

Next row—Increase
First size: rib 5, *m1, rib 4; rep from * to the last 5 sts; m1, rib 5—161 sts.
Second size: (m1, rib 3) 9 times, *m1, rib 4; rep from * to the last 27 sts; (m1, rib 3) 9 times—177 sts.

Change to size 7(4½mm) needles and work chevron patt as follows:
Row 1 (right side): *k1, m1, (k1, p1) 3 times, sl2tog knitwise, k1, p2sso, (p1, k1) 3 times, m1; rep from * to the last st; k1.
Row 2: k8, *p1, k15; rep from * to the last 9 sts; p1, k8.
Row 3: *k1, m1, (p1, k1) 3 times, sl2tog knitwise, k1, p2sso, (k1, p1) 3 times, m1, rep from * to the last st; k1.
Row 4: as row 2.

Rep rows 1 through 4 until back measures 10/10½in(25.5/27cm) from beg, with right side facing for next row.

Break off natural and, with gray, continue in patt as set until back measures 16/16½in(41/42cm) from beg. Place a marker at each end of row to mark beg of armholes. Continue in gray until back measures 19/20in(48.5/51cm) from beg, with right side facing for next row.

Break off gray and, with charcoal, continue as set until back measures 22½/23½in(57/59.5cm) from beg, with right side facing for next row.***

Change to size 6(4mm) needles, and k1, p1 rib (right-side rows having a k1 at each end, wrong-side rows having a p1 at each end) for 4½in(11.5cm), ending with right side facing for next row.

Shape shoulders
Working in rib, bind off 18/20 sts at beg of next 6 rows.
Bind off the rem 53/57 sts (back neck).

FRONT
Work as for back from ** to ***.

Change to size 6(4mm) needles and k1, p1 rib as for back, for 2in(5cm), ending with right side facing for next row.

Shape neck
Rib 62/69 sts; bind off the next 37/39 sts (front neck); place the rem sts on a spare needle.

Turn and rib these first 62/69 sts, decreasing 1 st at neck edge of next 3 rows. Rib 1 row straight, then dec 1 st at neck edge of next and every foll alt row until 54/60 sts rem. Continue straight in rib until piece corresponds in length with back at shoulder, with right side facing for next row.

Shoulders

Working in rib, bind off 18/20 stitches at beg of next and foll 2 right-side rows, thus binding off all sts.

With right side facing, rejoin yarn to sts on spare needle, and rib to end of row. Dec 1 st at neck edge of next 3 rows. Rib 1 row straight, then dec 1 st at neck edge of next and every foll alt row until 54/60 sts rem. Continue straight in rib until piece corresponds in length with back at shoulder, with wrong side facing for next row.

Working in rib, bind off 18/20 sts at beg of next and foll 2 wrong-side rows, thus binding off all sts.

SLEEVES

With size 5(3¾mm) needles and natural, cast on 66 sts. K1, p1 rib for 3in(8cm).

Next row—Increase

Rib 3, *m1, rib 2; rep from* to the last 3 sts; m1, rib 3—97 sts.

Change to size 7(4½mm) needles and work chevron patt as back for 3 rows. Working in chevron patt as set, inc at each side of sleeve as follows:

Row 4 (wrong side): k1, m1, patt as back to the last st; m1, k1.
Row 5: k1, patt as back to the last st, k1.
Row 6: k1, patt as back to the last st; k1.
Row 7: k1, m1, patt as back to the last st; m1, k1.
Row 8: k2, patt as back to the last 2 sts; k2.
Row 9: k2tog, m1, patt as back to the last 2 sts; m1, ssk.

Row 10: as row 8.
Row 11: k1, p1, m1, patt as back to the last 2 sts; m1, p1, k1.
Row 12: k3, patt as back to the last 3 sts; k3.
Row 13: k2tog, k1, m1, patt as back to the last 3 sts; m1, k1, ssk.
Row 14: as row 12.
Row 15: p1, k1, p1, m1, patt as back to the last 3 sts; m1, p1, k1, p1.
Row 16: k4, patt as back to the last 4 sts; k4.
Row 17: k2tog, p1, k1, m1, patt as back to the last 4 sts; m1, k1, p1, ssk.
Row 18: as row 16.
Row 19: (k1, p1) twice, m1, patt as back to the last 4 sts; m1, (p1, k1) twice.
Row 20: k5, patt as back to the last 5 sts; k5.
Row 21: k2tog, k1, p1, k1, m1, patt as back to the last 5 sts; m1, k1, p1, k1, ssk.
Row 22: as row 20.
Row 23: (p1, k1) twice, p1, m1, patt as back to the last 5 sts; m1, p1 (k1, p1) twice.
Row 24: k6, patt as back to the last 6 sts; k6.
Row 25: k2tog, (p1, k1) twice, m1, patt as back to the last 6 sts; m1, (k1, p1) twice, ssk.
Row 26: as row 24.
Row 27: (k1, p1) 3 times, m1, patt as back to the last 6 sts; m1, (p1, k1) 3 times.
Row 28: k7, patt as back to the last 7 sts; k7.
Row 29: k2tog, (k1, p1) twice, k1, m1, patt as back to the last 7 sts; m1, k1, (p1, k1) twice, ssk.
Row 30: as row 28.
Row 31: (p1, k1) 3 times, p1, m1, patt as back to the last 7 sts; m1, p1 (k1, p1) 3 times.

Textured Chevron Sweater

Dropped shoulder

rib collar.

Textured chevron stitch.

1x1 rib hem & cuffs.

Continue in this manner, working all increased sts in k on wrong-side rows, and working a k2tog at beg and an ssk at end of next right-side and every foll fourth row. Keeping continuity, work increased sts in rib on right-side rows.

When sleeve measures 10/10½in(25.5/27cm) from beg, with right side facing for next row, break off natural and continue as set in gray, until there are 147/151 sts.

Patt 1 row. Change to size 6(4mm) needles and charcoal and continue straight in k1, p1 rib as for back until sleeve measures 20/20½(51/52cm) from beg. Bind off all sts in rib.

COLLAR
With size 5(3¾mm) needles and charcoal, cast on 125/131 sts. K1, p1 rib (right-side rows having a k1 at each end, wrong-side rows having a p1 at each end) for 1in(2.5cm).

Change to size 7(4½mm) needles and patt as follows:
Row 1 (right side): *k1, p1; rep from * to the last st; k1.
Row 2: knit.
Rep these 2 rows until collar measures 4in(10cm) from beg, with wrong side facing for next row. Bind off all sts loosely and evenly in knit.

FINISHING
Do not press garment pieces.

Sew back and front together at shoulder seams.

Place center of cast-on edge of collar at center back of neck, and cast-on ends of collar at center front of neck. Sew collar around neck, loosely and evenly.

Place center top of sleeves at shoulder seams, and sew sleeves to body between markers. Sew up side and sleeve seams.

Mohair Cardigan

In Lewis, a day without wind is a rarity, so there is always a certain magic in the few occasions when the moorland lochs are still enough to reflect the sky. This loch has no name, although it certainly deserves one. I picked out its evening shades and atmosphere in this light, casual throw-on cardigan with slip-stitch stripes.

RATING ●

Mohair Cardigan

SIZES
To fit chest
38/40/42/44in(97/102/107/112cm)

KNITTED MEASUREMENTS
Chest 44½/46½/48½/50½in(113/118/123/128cm)
Length from top of shoulder
30/31/31½/32in(76.5/79/80/81.5cm)
Sleeve length
20/20/20½/20½in(51/51/52/52cm)

MATERIALS
Standard mohair yarn, 138yds per 1¾oz(125m per 50g):
4/5/5/5 1¾oz(50g) balls in dark navy; 3 1¾oz(50g) balls in dusk blue; 2 1¾oz(50g) balls in cloud gray; 1/1/1/2 1¾oz(50g) balls in honey gold; 1 1¾oz(50g) ball in light lemon.
1 pair each size 6(4mm) and size 9(5½mm) needles
1 stitch holder
Stitch markers

GAUGE
8 sts and 12 rows to 2in(5cm) measured over patt, using size 9(5½mm) needles. To work a gauge swatch, cast on 21 sts and patt as for back.

BACK
With size 6(4mm) needles and dark navy, cast on 84/88/92/96 sts. K1, p1 rib for 3¾/4/4/4in(9.5/10/10/10cm).

Next row—Increase
K2, *m1, k20/21/22/23; rep from * to the last 2 sts; m1, k2—89/93/97/101 sts.

Change to size 9(5½mm) needles and p 1 row. Then joining in and breaking off colors as required, patt as follows:
Row 1: with dusk blue, k1, *sl3 purlwise with yarn at back, k1; rep from * to end of row.
Row 2: with dusk blue, p2, *sl1 purlwise with yarn at front, p3; rep from * to the last 3 sts; sl1 purlwise with yarn at front, p2.
Row 3: with dusk blue, knit.
Row 4: with dusk blue, purl.
Row 5: with light lemon, as row 1.
Row 6: with honey gold, as row 2.
Row 7: with cloud gray, as row 3.
Row 8: with cloud gray, as row 4.
Rows 9–12: with dark navy, as rows 1 through 4.

Rep rows 1 through 12 until back measures 19¼/20/20¼/20½in(49/51/51.5/52cm) from beg. Place a marker at each end of row, then continue straight in patt until back measures 30/31/31½/32in(76.5/79/80/81.5cm) from beg, with right side facing for next row.

Shape shoulders
Keeping continuity of patt, bind off 8 sts at beg of next 6 rows. Then bind off 5/7/8/10 sts at beg of next 2 rows, and place the rem 31/31/33/33 sts on a holder for back neck.

Right front
With size 6(4mm) needles and dark navy, cast on 38/40/42/44 sts. K1, p1 rib for 3¾/4/4/4in(9.5/10/10/10cm).

Next row—Increase
K19/20/21/22, m1, k19/20/21/22—39/41/43/45 sts.

Change to size 9(5½mm) needles and p 1 row. Joining in and breaking off colors as required, patt as follows:

First and third sizes only
Row 1: with dusk blue, k2, *sl3 purlwise with yarn at back, k1; rep from * to the last st; k1.
Row 2: with dusk blue, p3, *sl1 purlwise with yarn at front, p3; rep from * to end of row.
Row 3: with dusk blue, knit.
Row 4: with dusk blue, purl.
Row 5: with light lemon, as row 1.
Row 6: with honey gold, as row 2.
Row 7: with cloud gray, as row 3.
Row 8: with cloud gray, as row 4.
Rows 9–12: With dark navy, as rows 1 through 4.

Rep rows 1 through 12.

Second and fourth sizes only
Patt as for back.

All sizes
Continue in patt as set until front measures 14/14½/14½/14½in(36/37/37/37cm) from beg, with right side facing for next row.††

Shape neck
**Next row: keeping continuity of patt, k2tog, patt to end of row.
Keeping continuity, patt 8 rows straight.
Next row: patt to the last 2 sts, p2tog.
Keeping continuity, patt 8 rows straight.

Rep from ** until 29/31/32/34 sts rem. **At the same time,** when the front measures 19¼/20/20¼/20½in(49/51/51.5/52cm) from beg, place a marker at unshaped edge of row.

Continue straight in patt until front corresponds in length with back at beg of shoulder bind-off, with wrong side facing for next row.

Shape shoulder
Keeping continuity of patt, bind off 8 sts and patt to end of row. Keeping continuity, patt 1 row straight. Rep these last 2 rows 2 more times. Bind off the rem 5/7/8/10 sts.

LEFT FRONT
Work as for right front to ††.

Shape neck
**Next row: patt to the last 2 sts, k2tog.
Keeping continuity, patt 8 rows straight.
Next row: keeping continuity, p2tog, patt to end of row.
Keeping continuity, patt 8 rows straight.

Rep from ** until 29/31/32/34 sts rem. **At the same time,** when front measures 19¼/20/20¼/20½in(49/51/51.5/52cm) place a marker at unshaped edge of row.

Continue straight in patt until front corresponds in length with back at beg of shoulder bind-off, with right side facing for next row.

Shape shoulder as for right front.

SLEEVES
With size 6(4mm) needles and dark navy, cast on 40/42/42/44 sts. K1, p1 rib for 3½in(9cm).

Next row—Increase
K4/1/1/2, *m1, k4/5/5/5; rep from * to the last 4/1/1/2 sts; m1, k4/1/1/2—49/51/51/53 sts.

Change to size 9(5½mm) needles and p 1 row.

Begin working in patt as for back/as for first & third size right front/as for first & third size right front/as for back, and keeping continuity of patt, inc 1 st at each end of fifth and every foll fifth row until there are 87/89/91/93 sts. Work all increased sts into patt.

Mohair
Cardigan

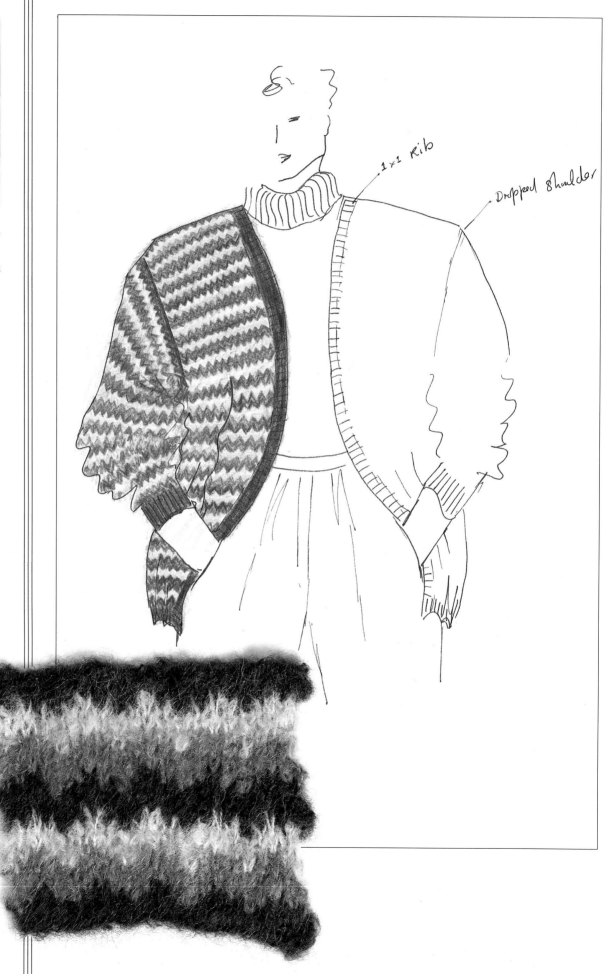

1 x 1 Rib

Dropped Shoulder

Continue straight in patt until sleeve measures 20/20/20½/20½in(51/51/52/52cm) from beg. Bind off all sts.

FINISHING
Sew right and left fronts to back at shoulders.

Right front band
With right side of right front facing, size 6(4mm) needles, and dark navy, knit up 149/155/157/159 sts along right front edge from beg of rib to back neck holder; then pick up and knit the first 15/15/16/16 sts from holder—164/170/173/175 sts.

K1, p1 rib (third and fourth sizes having a k1 at each end of wrong-side rows and a p1 at each end of right-side rows) for 2½in(6cm). Bind off evenly in rib.

Left front band
With right side of back facing, size 6(4mm) needles, and dark navy, pick up and knit the rem sts from back neck holder; then knit up 149/155/157/159 sts along left front edge—165/171/174/176 sts.

K1, p1 rib (first and second sizes having a k1 at each end of wrong-side rows and a p1 at each end of right-side rows) for 2½in(6cm). Bind off evenly in rib.

Sew up rib seam at center back neck.

Place center top of sleeves at shoulder seams and sew sleeves to body between markers. Sew up side and sleeve seams.

Norwegian Style Sweater

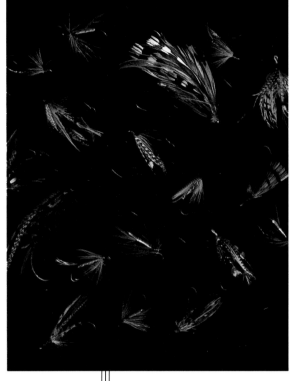

With hundreds of moorland lochs to choose from, it is little wonder that Lewis men—and a few Lewis women—are keen anglers. **T**he effect of bright fishing flies on deep, dark, peaty water is beautifully captured with the Norwegian Flea Pattern, black fleck yarn, and vibrant patterns on the yoke. **A**nother easy, loose style for casual days.

RATING ● ●

Norwegian Style Sweater

SIZES
To fit chest 38/40/42/44in(97/102/107/112cm)

KNITTED MEASUREMENTS
Chest 44/46/48/50in(112/117/122/127cm)
Length from top of shoulder 26½/27/27½/28in(67.5/68.5/70/71cm)
Sleeve length 19½/20/20½/21in(49.5/51/52/53.5cm)

MATERIALS
13/13/14/14 1¾oz(50g) balls of DK fleck yarn 73yds per oz(120m per 50g)
1 1¾oz(50g) ball of DK yarn in each of 6 solid contrasting colors 70yds per oz(115m per 50g)
1 pair each size 4(3½mm), size 6(4mm) and size 7(4½mm) needles
2 stitch holders
Stitch markers

GAUGE
24 sts and 32 rows to 4in(10cm) measured over st st, using size 6(4mm) needles.

BACK
**With size 4(3½mm) needles and fleck yarn, cast on 114/120/126/130 sts. K1, p1 rib for 3in(8cm).

Next row—Increase
Rib 1/4/7/2, *m1, rib 7; rep from * to the last 1/4/7/2 sts; m1, rib 1/4/7/2—131/137/143/149 sts.

Change to size 6(4mm) needles and continue straight in st st until back measures 14/14¼/14½/14½in(35.5/36/37/37cm) from beg, with right side facing for next row.

Change to size 7(4½mm) needles and, joining in and breaking off colors as required, work the patt from chart, repeating the 24 patt sts 5/5/5/6 times, and working the first 5/8/11/2 sts and the last 6/9/12/3 sts on right-side rows, and the first 6/9/12/3 sts and the last 5/8/11/2 sts on wrong-side rows, as indicated on chart.

Continue in this manner, and when back measures 16/16¼/16½/16½ in(41/41.5/42/42cm) from beg, place a marker at each end of row to mark beg of armholes.***

Continue working chart as set, working the first 28 rows once only, and thereafter repeating rows 29 through 40 until back measures 26½/27/27½/28in(67.5/68.5/70/71cm) from beg, with right side facing for next row.

Shape shoulders
With fleck yarn, bind off 43/45/47/49 sts; k the next 45/47/49/51 sts and place these sts on a holder for back neck; patt the rem sts.
Next row: bind off the rem sts.

FRONT
Work as for back from ** to ***.

Continue working chart as set, working the first 28 rows once only, and thereafter repeating rows 29 through 40 until armholes measure 7½/7¾/7¾/8¼in(19/19.5/19.5/21cm).

Shape neck
Keeping continuity, patt 52/54/56/58 sts; place the next 27/29/31/33 sts on a holder for front neck; place the rem sts on a spare needle.

†Turn, and keeping continuity of patt, work the 52/54/56/58 sts, decreasing 1 st at neck edge of next 3 rows. Patt 1 row straight, then dec 1 st at neck edge of next and every foll alt row until 43/45/47/49 sts rem. Then continue straight in patt until armhole corresponds in length with that of back. Bind off all sts.††

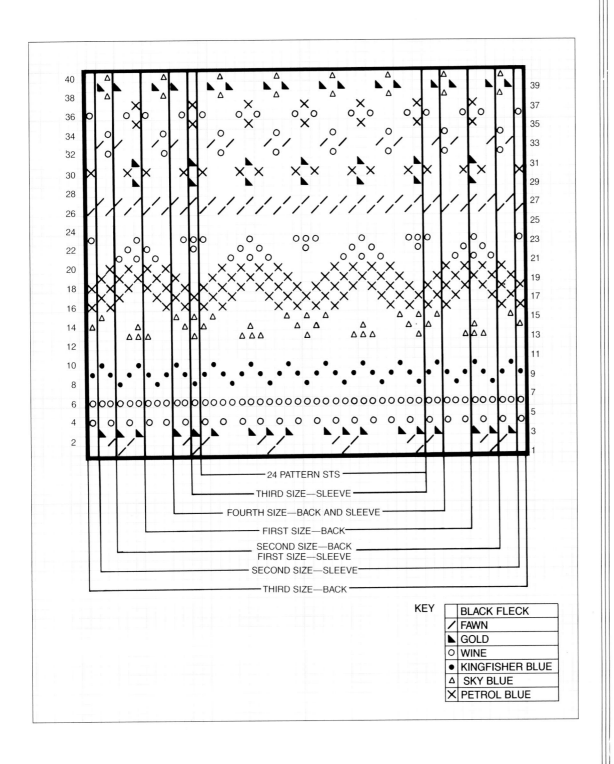

24 PATTERN STS

THIRD SIZE—SLEEVE

FOURTH SIZE—BACK AND SLEEVE

FIRST SIZE—BACK

SECOND SIZE—BACK
FIRST SIZE—SLEEVE

SECOND SIZE—SLEEVE

THIRD SIZE—BACK

KEY

	BLACK FLECK
/	FAWN
◣	GOLD
○	WINE
●	KINGFISHER BLUE
△	SKY BLUE
✕	PETROL BLUE

Norwegian Style Sweater

1×1 rib crew neck

Flea Pattern

Dropped shoulder.

1×1 rib hem & cuffs.

Rejoin appropriate yarns to the sts on spare needle and, keeping continuity, patt to end of row. Then complete as previous side, working from † to ††.

SLEEVES

With size 4(3½mm) needles and fleck yarn, cast on 56/58/60/62 sts. K1, p1 rib for 3in(8cm).

Next row—Increase

Rib 3/4/5/6, *m1, rib 5; rep from * to the last 3/4/5/6 sts; m1, rib 3/4/5/6—67/69/71/73 sts.

Change to size 6(4mm) needles and work in st st, increasing 1 st at each end of every fifth row 6 times. Then continue in st st and inc 1 st at each end of every foll fourth row until there are 113/117/121/125 sts in total.

Change to size 7(4½mm) needles and work the patt from chart, repeating the 24 patt sts 4/4/5/5 times, and working the first 8/10/0/2 sts and the last 9/11/1/3 sts on right-side rows, and the first 9/11/1/3 sts and the last 8/10/0/2 sts on wrong-side rows, as indicated on chart.

Continue increasing 1 st at each end of every fourth row, working all increased sts into patt, until there are 125/129/131/137 sts in total. Work straight to row 28 of chart. Bind off all sts.

FINISHING

Press pieces very lightly on wrong side, omitting ribs. Sew back and front together at left shoulder.

Neckband

With size 4(3½mm) needles and fleck yarn, pick up and knit the 45/47/49/51 sts from back neck holder; knit up 17/17/18/18 sts to front neck holder; pick up and knit the 27/29/31/33 sts from front neck holder; knit up 17/17/18/18 sts to top of shoulder—106/110/116/120 sts. K1, p1 rib for 2in(5cm). Break off fleck and rib for a further 2in(5cm) in a contrasting color. Bind off all sts loosely and evenly.

Sew up right shoulder and neckband seam. Turn neckband in half to the inside and slip stitch in position.

Place center top of sleeves at shoulder seams and sew sleeves in position between markers. Press seams lightly on wrong side, omitting neckband rib.

Sew up side and sleeve seams. Press seams lightly on wrong side, omitting ribs.

Moss Rib Sweater

From a distance, the moorland gives the appearance of a constant sweep of grass and heather. The eye is deceived, however, for look closely and there are dozens of species of sphagnum moss and other wetland plants. I don't know the name of this one, but its rich red color is particularly spectacular in autumn. I picked the deepest shade of red from the very heart of the plant and used it in a warm, outdoor sweater in a simple but highly appropriate moss rib.

RATING ●

Moss Rib Sweater

SIZES
To fit chest 38/40/42/44in(97/102/107/112cm)

KNITTED MEASUREMENTS
Chest 44/46/48/50in(112/117/122/127cm)
Length from top of shoulder 26½/27/27½/28in(67.5/68.5/70/71cm)
Sleeve length (cuff to underarm) 19/19/19½/19½in(48.5/48.5/50/50cm)

MATERIALS
12/12/13/13 3½oz(100g) balls of bulky yarn, approx. 110yds per 3½oz(100m per 100g)
1 pair each size 8(5mm), size 9(5½mm), and size 10(6mm) needles
1 stitch holder

GAUGE
8 sts and 11 rows to 2in(5cm) measured over patt, using size 10(6mm) needles.

BACK
**With size 8(5mm) needles, cast on 80/84/88/92 sts. K2, p2 rib for 3½in(9cm).

Next row—Increase
Rib 4/2/4/2, *m1, rib 9/10/10/11; rep from * to the last 4/2/4/2 sts; m1, rib 4/2/4/2—89/93/97/101 sts.
Change to size 10(6mm) needles and patt as follows:
Row 1: *p1, k3; rep from * to the last st; p1.
Row 2: k2, *p1, k3; rep from * to the last 3 sts; p1, k2.

Rep rows 1 and 2.

Continue in patt until back measures 16½/17/17/17½in(42/43/43/44.5cm) from beg.

Shape armholes
Keeping continuity of patt, shape as follows: bind off 3 sts at beg of next 2 rows. Bind off 2 sts at beg of next 2 rows. Dec 1 st at each end of next row. Patt 1 row straight. Dec 1 st at each end of next row.

Rep the last 2 rows once more—73/77/81/85 sts rem.***

Continue straight in patt until armhole measures 10/10/10½/10½in(25.5/25.5/27/27cm).

Shape shoulders
Keeping continuity of patt, shape as follows: bind off 6/7/7/8 sts at beg of next 2 rows. Bind off 7/7/8/8 sts at beg of next 2 rows. Bind off 7/8/8/9 sts at beg of next 2 rows. Place the rem 33/33/35/35 sts on a holder (back neck).

FRONT
Work as for back from ** to ***.
Patt 2/2/4/4 rows straight.

Shape neck
Patt 27/29/30/32 sts and place these sts on a spare needle; bind off the next 19/19/21/21 sts (center front neck); keeping continuity, patt the rem 27/29/30/32 sts.

†††Keeping continuity, patt these 27/29/30/32 sts, decreasing 1 st at neck edge of fourth row. Then continue decreasing 1 st at neck edge of every foll sixth row until 20/22/23/25 sts rem.

Continue straight in patt until armhole corresponds in length with that of back, with armhole edge at beg for next row.

Shape shoulder
Keeping continuity of patt, shape as follows: bind off 6/7/7/8 sts at beg of next row. Patt 1 row straight. Bind off 7/7/8/8 sts at beg of next row. Patt 1 row straight. Bind off the rem 7/8/8/9 sts.††††

Beg at neck edge, rejoin yarn to the sts on spare needle and complete as previous side, working from ††† to ††††.

SLEEVES

With size 6(5mm) needles, cast on 40/40/44/44 sts. K2, p2 rib for 3in(8cm).

Next row—Increase

Rib 4/4/2/2; *m1, rib 4/4/5/5; rep from * to the last 4/4/2/2 sts; m1, rib 4/4/2/2—49/49/53/53 sts.

Change to size 10(6mm) needles and patt as back, increasing 1 st at each end of third row. Then inc 1 st at each end of every foll fifth row until there are 81/81/85/85 sts. Work all increased sts into patt.

Continue straight in patt until sleeve measures 19/19/19½/19½in(48.5/48.5/50/50cm).

Shape top

Keeping continuity of patt, shape as follows: bind off 3 sts at beg of next 6 rows. Bind off 4 sts at beg of next 4 rows. Bind off 6 sts at beg of next 2 rows. Bind off the rem sts.

FINISHING

Pin out garment pieces to size and press pieces lightly, omitting k2, p2 ribs.
Sew back and front together at shoulders.

COLLAR

With size 9(5½mm) needles, and right side of work facing, knit up 44/44/45/45 sts up right front neck edge, from end of front neck bind-off to shoulder seam; then pick up and knit the first 16/16/17/17 sts from back neck holder—60/60/62/62 sts total. K2, p2 rib (third and fourth sizes having a k2 at each end of wrong-side rows and a p2 at each end of right-side rows) until collar fits across front neck bind-off. Bind off all sts loosely and evenly in rib.

With size 9(5½mm) needles, and right side of work facing, pick up and knit the rem sts from back neck holder, knitting the first 2 sts together(16/16/17/17 sts rem); then knit up 44/44/45/45 sts down left neck edge from shoulder seam to beg of front neck bind-off. Complete as previous side.

Sew right and left collar at center back. Sew front end of right collar along front neck bind-off, then place front end of left collar on top and stitch in position.

Fold sleeves in half lengthwise and mark center top. Place center top of sleeves at shoulder seams and sew sleeves into armholes.

Sew up side and sleeve seams. Press seams lightly on wrong side, omitting ribs.

The Atlantic Coast

Shawl Collar Sweater

Unlike the sheltered sand at Broad Bay, the beach at Dalmore on the western coast of Lewis resounds with the raw power of the Atlantic. That power is evident in the large sea-worn boulders, tossed and piled at the head of the beach as if they were small pieces of shingle. I chose a marled yarn to match the texture and color of these rocks and designed a warm, casual sweater with a simple pattern.

RATING ● ●

Shawl Collar Sweater

SIZES

To fit chest 38–40/42–44in(97–102/107–112cm)

KNITTED MEASUREMENTS

Chest 45¼/48in(115/122cm)
Length from top of shoulder 26/27in(66/68.5cm)
Sleeve length (cuff to underarm) 19/19½in(48.5/50cm)

MATERIALS

17/18 1¾oz(50g) balls of sportweight yarn, 110yds per 1¾oz(100m per 50g)
1 pair each size 5(3¾mm) and size 7(4½mm) needles
2 stitch holders

GAUGE

12 sts and 14 rows to 2in(5cm) measured over patt, using size 7(4½mm) needles. To work a gauge swatch, cast on 24 sts and patt as back.

BACK

**With size 5(3¾mm) needles, cast on 114/120 sts. K1, p1 rib for 3in(8cm).

Next row—Increase

Rib 4/2, *m1, rib 5; rep from * to the last 5/3 sts; m1, rib 5/3—136/144 sts.

Change to size 7(4½mm) needles and patt as follows:
Row 1 (right side): knit.
Row 2: purl.
Row 3: p3, *miss next st and knit into second st, then knit into missed st and slip both sts from needle together (i.e., twist 2), p2; rep from * to the last 5 sts; twist 2, p3.
Row 4: k3, *p2, k2; rep from * to the last 3 sts; k3.
Rows 5 & 6: as rows 3 & 4.
Rows 7 & 8: as rows 1 & 2.
Row 9: p1, *twist 2, p2; rep from * to the last 3 sts; twist 2, p1.
Row 10: k1, *p2, k2; rep from * to the last 3 sts: p2, k1.
Rows 11 & 12: as rows 9 & 10.

Rep rows 1 through 12.

Continue straight in patt until back measures 16/16½in(41/42cm), with right side facing for next row.

Shape armholes

Keeping continuity of patt, shape as follows: bind off 4 sts at beg of next 2 rows. Bind off 2 sts at beg of next 2 rows. Dec 1 st at each end of next row. Patt 1 row straight, then dec 1 st at each end of next and every foll alt row until 112/120 sts rem.***

Continue straight in patt until armhole measures 10/10½in(25.5/27cm), with right side facing for next row.

Shape shoulders

Keeping continuity of patt, shape as follows: bind off 10/11 sts at beg of next 2 rows. Bind off 11 sts at beg of next 2 rows. Bind off 11/12 sts at beg of next 2 rows. Place the rem 48/52 sts on a holder (back neck).

FRONT

Work as for back from ** to***.

Continue straight in patt until armhole measures 7¾/8in(19.5/20cm), with right side facing for next row.

Shape neck

Patt 42/45 sts; place the next 28/30 sts on a holder (center front neck); place the rem sts on a spare needle.

†Keeping continuity of patt, work these 42/45 sts, decreasing 1 st at neck edge of next 5 rows. Patt 1 row straight, then dec 1 st at neck edge of next and every foll alt row until 32/34 sts rem.††

When armhole corresponds in length with that of back, and with right side facing for next row, shape shoulder as follows: bind off 10/11 sts, patt to end of row. Patt 1 row straight. Bind off 11 sts, patt to end of row. Patt 1 row straight. Bind off the rem 11/12 sts.

With right side of work facing, rejoin yarn to the 42/45 sts on spare needle, and keeping continuity, patt to end of row. Then work as previous side from † to ††.

When armhole corresponds in length with that of back, and with wrong side facing for next row, shape shoulder as for previous side.

SLEEVES
With size 5(3¾mm) needles, cast on 58/62 sts. K1, p1 rib for 3in(8cm).

Next row—Increase
Rib 3/5, *m1, rib 4; rep from * to the last 3/5 sts; m1, rib 3/5—72/76 sts.

Change to size 7(4½mm) needles and patt as back, increasing 1 st at each end of fifth row. Then inc 1 st at each end of every foll fourth row until there are 120/126 sts.

Continue straight in patt until sleeve measures 19/19½in(48.5/50cm) from beg, with right side facing for next row.

Shape top
Keeping continuity of patt, bind off 4 sts at beg of next 8 rows. Bind off 8 sts at beg of next 6 rows. Bind off rem sts.

FINISHING
Do not press garment pieces.

Sew back and front together at left shoulder seam.

Neck rib
With size 5(3¾mm) needles, pick up and knit the 48/52 sts from back neck holder; knit up 18/19 sts to front neck holder; pick up and knit the 28/30 sts from front neck holder; knit up 18/19 sts to top of right shoulder—112/120 sts. K1, p1 rib for 6 rows. Bind off evenly in rib.

Sew up right shoulder and neck rib seam. Press shoulder seams lightly on wrong side, omitting rib.

Collar
With size 5(3¾mm) needles, cast on 132/142 sts. K1, p1 rib for 2 rows, then continue in rib as set and bind off 1 st at beg of next 30/34 rows. Bind off the rem sts.

Sew bound-off edge and sides of collar loosely to inside of neck rib pick-up line, placing center of collar at center back neck and overlapping sides of collar along front neck.

Place center top of sleeves at shoulder seams and sew sleeves into armholes. Press seams lightly on wrong side.

Sew up side and sleeve seams. Press seams lightly on wrong side, omitting ribs.

Openwork Cotton Sweater

The Atlantic Ocean also has its quieter moods, as in summer, when it sometimes shimmers over clean, white sand, producing a wonderful turquoise color. I lifted that color directly and used it in this bright, casual sweater. The cool, lightweight stitch makes it perfect for summer wear.

RATING ● ●

Openwork Cotton Sweater

SIZES
To fit chest
38/40/42/44in(97/102/107/112cm)

KNITTED MEASUREMENTS
Chest 43/45/47/49in(110/115/119/125cm)
Length from top of shoulder
26½/27/27½/28in(67.5/68.5/70/71cm)
Sleeve length
18½/19/19/19½in(47/48.5/48.5/49.5cm)

MATERIALS
15/15/16/16 1¾oz(50g) balls of mercerized pearl cotton, 93yds per 1¾oz(85m per 50g)
1 pair each size 4(3½mm), 5(3¾mm), and 6(4mm) needles
3 buttons
Stitch holders
Stitch markers

GAUGE
Because of the lateral stretch of the patt, gauge must be determined by working a swatch as follows:

With size 6(4mm) needles, cast on 20 sts.
Row 1: k1, *yo, k2tog; rep from * to the last st; k1.
Row 2 & all foll rows: as row 1, working the yo of previous row as second st of k2tog.

Work 12 rows in total. Bind off all sts. Lay the swatch flat, **without stretching**, and measure with a ruler. The finished swatch should measure 3½in(9cm) in width, and 2in(5cm) in length.

BACK
With size 4(3½mm) needles, cast on 112/116/120/126 sts. K1, p1 rib for 2¾in(7cm).

Next row—Increase
First size: m1, rib 8, *m1, rib 16; rep from * to the last 8 sts; m1, rib 8—120 sts.
Second size: rib 4, *m1, rib 12; rep from * to the last 4 sts; m1, rib 4—126 sts.
Third size: rib 1, *m1, rib 13; rep from * to the last 2 sts; m1, rib 2—130 sts.
Fourth size: m1, rib 7, *m1, rib 14; rep from * to the last 7 sts; m1, rib 7—136 sts.

Change to size 6(4mm) needles and work openwork patt as given for gauge swatch, and continue straight in patt until back measures 16¼/16½/16¾/17in(41.5/42/42.5/43cm) from beg. Place markers for armholes at each end of last row.††

Continue in patt as set until armhole measures 9¼/9½/9¾/10in(23.5/24/25/25.5cm).

Shape neck and shoulders
Next row: patt 41/43/45/47(counting yo's as sts); leave the rem sts on a spare needle. Turn and shape the 41/43/45/47 sts of right shoulder as follows:
Row 1: p2tog, *yo, k2tog; rep from * to the last st; k1—40/42/44/46 sts rem.
Row 2: k1, *yo, k2tog; rep from * to the last 3 sts; k1, k2tog—39/41/43/45 sts rem.
Row 3: as row 1—38/40/42/44 sts rem.
Row 4: k1, *yo, k2tog; rep from * to the last st; k1.
Row 5: p2tog, k1, *yo, k2tog; rep from * to the last st, k1—37/39/41/43 sts rem.
Row 6: k1, *yo, k2tog; rep from * to end of row.

Bind off the 37/39/41/43 sts of right shoulder.

Place the next (center back) 38/40/40/42 sts on a holder for back neck.

With right side facing, rejoin yarn to the rem 41/43/45/47 sts of left shoulder and, beg at neck edge, shape as follows:
Row 1: k2, *yo, k2tog; rep from * to the last st, k1.
Row 2: k1, *yo, k2tog; rep from * to the last 2 sts; p2tog—40/42/44/46 sts rem.
Row 3: k2tog, k1, *yo, k2tog; rep from * to the last st; k1—39/41/43/45 sts rem.
Row 4: as row 2—38/40/42/44 sts rem.
Row 5: k1, *yo, k2tog; rep from * to the last st; k1.

Row 6: k1, *yo, k2tog; rep from * to the last 3 sts; k2tog, p1—37/39/41/43 sts rem.

Row 7: k2, *yo, k2tog; rep from * to the last st; k1. Bind off the 37/39/41/43 sts of left shoulder.

FRONT

Work as for back to ††. Then continue in patt as set until armhole measures 1½/1¾/1¾/2in(4/4.5/4.5/5cm).

First and fourth sizes only—Left front opening

Next row: k1, *yo, k2tog; rep from * 27/31 times; k1 (56/64 sts, counting yo's as sts); place the rem sts on a spare needle. Turn, and continue working these 56/64 sts of left front in patt as set, for 6in(15.5cm), ending with wrong side facing for next row.

Shape left neck

†††K1, *yo, k2tog; rep from * 3/4 times; k1. Place these 8/10 sts on a holder for front neck; k1, *yo, k2tog; rep from * to the last st; k1.

Second and third sizes only—Left front opening

Patt 59/61 sts, counting yo's as sts; place the rem sts on a spare needle.

Patt the 59/61 sts of left front as follows:

Row 1: *yo, k2tog; rep from * to the last st; k1.

Row 2: k1, *yo, k2tog; rep from * to end of row.

Rep these 2 rows for 6in(15.5cm), ending with wrong side facing for next row.

Shape left neck

†††(yo, k2tog) 4 times; k1. Place these 9 sts on a holder for front neck; k1, *yo, k2tog; rep from * to the last st; k1.

All sizes

Dec for neck shaping as follows:

Row 1 (right side): k1, *yo, k2tog; rep from * to the last 3 sts; k1, k2tog—47/49/51/53 sts rem.

Row 2: p2tog, *yo, k2tog; rep from * to the last st; k1—46/48/50/52 sts rem.

Row 3: as row 1—45/47/49/51 sts rem.

Row 4: as row 2—44/46/48/50 sts rem.

Row 5: as row 1—43/45/47/49 sts rem.

Row 6: as row 2—42/44/46/48 sts rem.

Row 7: k1, *yo, k2tog; rep from * to the last st; k1.

Row 8: p2tog, k1, *yo, k2tog; rep from * to the last st; k1—41/43/45/47 sts rem.

Row 9: k1, *yo, k2tog; rep from * to end of row.

Row 10: p2tog, *yo, k2tog; rep from * to the last st; k1—40/42/44/46 sts rem.

Row 11: as row 7.

Row 12: as row 8—39/41/43/45 sts rem.

Row 13: as row 9.

Row 14: as row 10—38/40/42/44 sts rem.

Row 15: as row 7.

Row 16: as row 8—37/39/41/43 sts rem.

First and second sizes only

Bind off shoulder sts.††††

Third and fourth sizes only

Row 17: as row 9.

Row 18: k2, *yo, k2tog; rep from * to the last st; k1.

Bind off shoulder sts.††††

All sizes—Right front opening

With right side facing, rejoin yarn to the sts on spare needle and bind off the next 8 sts (center front); patt the rem 56/59/61/64 sts as follows:

First and fourth sizes only

K1, *yo, k2tog; rep from * to the last st; k1. Rep this row until right front opening corresponds in length with left, with **right side** facing for next row. Then shape right neck, dec neck (working row 1 of neck dec on **wrong side**), and complete as left neck from ††† to ††††.

1x1 Rib
3 button open neck.

Dropped

Second and third sizes only
Row 1: *yo, k2tog; rep from * to the last st; k1.
Row 2: k1, *yo, k2tog; rep from * to end of row.
Rep these 2 rows until right opening corresponds in length with left, with **right side** facing for next row. Then shape right neck, dec neck (working row 1 of neck dec on **wrong side**), and complete as left neck from ††† to ††††.

SLEEVES (ALL SIZES)
With size 4(3½mm) needles, cast on 50/52/54/56 sts. K1, p1 rib for 2¾in(7cm).

Next row—Increase
First size: rib 2, *m1, rib 5; rep from * to the last 3 sts; m1, rib 3—60 sts.
Second size: rib 3, *m1, rib 5; rep from * to the last 4 sts; m1, rib 4—62 sts.
Third size: m1, rib 3, *m1, rib 6; rep from * to the last 3 sts; m1, rib 3—64 sts.
Fourth size: rib 1, *m1, rib 6; rep from * to the last st; m1, rib 1—66 sts.

Change to size 6(4mm) needles and work openwork patt for 2 rows. Then shape sleeve by increasing 1 st at each end of next and every foll third row as follows:
Row 1: m1, k1, *yo, k2tog; rep from * to the last st; m1, k1.
Rows 2 & 3: k2, *yo, k2tog; rep from * to the last 2 sts; k2.
Row 4: m1, k2, *yo, k2tog; rep from * to the last 2 sts; k1, m1, k1.
Rows 5 & 6: k1, *yo, k2tog; rep from * to the last st; k1.

Rep rows 1 through 6 until there are 106/108/110/110 sts. Then continue in this manner, but increasing 1 st at each end of every foll fourth row until there are 116/118/120/122 sts. Continue straight in patt until sleeve measures 18½/19/19/19½in(47/48.5/48.5/49.5cm) from beg.

Bind off all sts.

FINISHING
Sew back and front together at shoulders. Fold sleeve in half lengthwise and mark center top. Place center sleeve top at shoulder seam and sew sleeves to body betwen armhole markers. Sew up side and sleeve seams.

Neckband
With right side facing and size 5(3¾mm) needles, pick up and knit the 8/9/9/10 sts from right front neck holder; knit up 13/13/15/15 sts to shoulder seam; knit up 5 sts to back neck holder; pick up and knit the 38/40/40/42 sts from back neck holder, decreasing 1 st at center back neck; knit up 5 sts to shoulder seam; knit up 13/13/15/15 sts to left front neck holder; pick up and knit the 8/9/9/10 sts from left front neck holder—89/93/97/101 sts. Work in rib as follows:
Row 1 (wrong side): *k1, p1; rep from * to the last st; k1.
Row 2: *p1, k1; rep from * to the last st; p1.
Rep these 2 rows 4 more times (10 rows total). Bind off loosely and evenly in rib.

Left front rib
With right side facing, size 5(3¾mm) needles, and beg at top of neckband rib, knit up 36 sts along left front opening. K1, p1 rib for 10 rows. Bind off loosely and evenly in rib.

Right front rib
With right side facing, beg at bottom of opening and work as left front opening for 5 rows.
Next row (right side): rib 6, (bind off next st then sl st back to left needle and ktog with foll st, rib 9) twice; bind off next st then sl st back to left needle and ktog with foll st, rib 3.
Next row: rib 4, cast on 2, (rib 10, cast on 2) twice, rib 6.
Rib 3 rows. Bind off loosely and evenly in rib.

Sew lower end of left front rib to bound-off sts of center front, then sew lower end of right front rib on top. Sew on buttons to correspond with buttonholes.

Cotton Raglan Sweater

As I took an autumn walk on Dal-more Beach, my eye was caught by the contrast between a piece of dried black seaweed and layers of banded sand. I took the colors and the effect for this slip stitch pattern, worked in narrow bands. The shape is loose and comfortable; the touch of black at the collar provides the contrast.

RATING ● ● ●

Cotton Raglan Sweater

SIZES
To fit chest
38/40/42/44in(97/102/107/112cm)

KNITTED MEASUREMENTS
Chest
44/45½/47/49in(112/116/120/125cm)
Length from top of shoulder
26½/27/27½/28in(67.5/68.5/70/71cm)
Sleeve length (cuff to underarm)
18/18½/18½/19in(46/47/47/48cm)

MATERIALS
Mercerized cotton yarn, 70yds per
1¾oz(63m per 50g): 7/7/8/8 1¾oz(50g)
balls in natural; 7/7/7/8 1¾oz(50g) balls in
gray; 8/8/9/9 1¾oz(50g) balls in sand; 1
1¾oz(50g) ball in black (optional).
1 pair each size 7(4½mm) and size
9(5½mm) needles
1 circular 16in(40cm) size 7(4½mm)
needle
4 stitch holders

GAUGE
9 sts and 14 rows to 2in(5cm) measured
over patt, using size 9(5½mm) needles.

BACK
**With size 7(4½mm) needles and sand,
cast on 86/90/94/98 sts. K1, p1 rib in alter-
nating stripes of 2 rows sand / 2 rows gray /
2 rows natural until rib measures
3in(8cm).

Next row—Increase
Rib 1/3/5/1, *m1, rib 7/7/7/8; rep from * to
the last 1/3/5/1 sts; m1, rib 1/3/5/1—99/
103/107/111 sts.

Change to size 9(5½mm) needles and patt
as follows (carry yarns not in use up side of
work):

Row 1 (right side): with sand, k1,*sl1
purlwise with yarn at front, k1; rep from *
to end of row.
Row 2: with sand, purl.
Row 3: with gray, k1, *sl1 purlwise with
yarn at back, k1; rep from * to end of row.
Row 4: with gray, purl.
Row 5: with natural, k1, *sl1 purlwise with
yarn at front, k1; rep from * to end of row.
Row 6: with natural, purl.
Rows 7 & 8: with sand, as rows 3 & 4.
Rows 9 & 10: with gray, as rows 1 & 2.
Rows 11 & 12: with natural, as rows 3 & 4.

Rep rows 1 through 12 until back measures
15½/15½/15½/15¾in(39.5/39.5/9.5/
40cm), with right side facing for next row.

Shape raglan
Keeping continuity of patt, bind off 3 sts
at beg of next 2 rows. Dec as follows:
##**Row 1:** k1, k2tog; keeping continuity,
patt to the last 3 sts; ssk, k1.
Row 2: purl.
Row 3: as row 1.
Row 4: purl.
Row 5: k2; keeping continuity, patt to
the last 2 sts; k2.
Row 6: purl.###

Rep these last 6 rows until 61/61/61/65 sts
rem.***
Then continue to dec as set at each end of
every foll alt row until 33/35/37/39 sts rem.
Place sts on a holder for back neck.

FRONT
Work for back from ** to ***

Keeping continuity of patt, continue to dec
as set at each end of every foll alt row until
55/57/59/61 sts rem, and wrong side faces
for next row.

Shape neck
P19; place the next 17/19/21/23 sts on a
holder for front neck; place the rem sts on a
spare needle.

†††Turn, and keeping continuity of patt, work these 19 sts, decreasing at raglan edge on every alt row as set, and decreasing 1 st at neck edge of first 3 rows then at every alt row, 5 times. Continue straight at neck edge and continue to dec at raglan edge until 1 st remains. Fasten off.††††

With wrong side facing, rejoin appropriate yarn and purl the 19 sts from spare needle. Then work as previous side from ††† to ††††.

SLEEVES

With size 7(4½mm) needles and sand, cast on 40/42/44/46 sts. K1, p1 rib in stripes as back for 3in(8cm).

Next row—Increase

Rib 4/1/2/3, *m1, rib 4/5/5/5; rep from * to the last 4/1/2/3 sts; m1, rib 4/1/2/3—49/51/53/55 sts.

Change to size 9(5½mm) needles and patt as back, increasing 1 st at each end of eighth row. Then inc 1 st at each end of every foll fourth row until there are 97/99/101/103 sts. Work all increased sts into patt.

Continue straight in patt until sleeve measures 18/18½/18½/19in(46/47/47/48cm), with right side facing for next row.

Shape raglan

Keeping continuity of patt, bind off 3 sts at beg of next 2 rows. Then dec as given for back from ## to ### and repeat the 6 rows until 59/57/55/57 sts rem. Then, keeping continuity of patt, continue to dec as set at each end of every foll alt row until 47 sts rem. P 1 row.

Mark the 5 center sts and, keeping continuity of patt as far as possible, continue to dec at each end of every alt row as set, and **at the same time** dec 1 st at each side of the 5 center sts on every alt row (working k2tog, patt 5, ssk) until 15/15/15/17 sts rem. Place sts on a holder.

Press pieces lightly on wrong side, omitting ribs. Join back, sleeves, and front at raglan seams. Press seams on wrong side.

Neckband

With circular size 7(4½mm) needle, sand yarn, and right side of garment facing, pick up and knit the 33/35/37/39 sts from back neck holder, decreasing 2 sts evenly; pick up and knit the 15/15/15/17 sts from sleeve holder, decreasing 1 st at center; knit up 15 sts to front neck holder; pick up and knit the 17/19/21/23 sts from front neck holder; knit up 15 sts to sleeve holder; pick up and knit the 15/15/15/17 sts from sleeve holder, decreasing 1 st at center—106/110/114/122 sts.

K1, p1 rib for 8 rows. Bind off loosely and evenly in rib.

Collar (optional)

With circular size 7(4½mm) needle and black, cast on 106/110/114/122 sts. St st for 3in(8cm). Bind off evenly.

With purl side of collar facing, slip stitch bound-off edge of collar around neck along rib pickup line, so that collar curls over neckband.

Sew up side and sleeve seams. Press seams on wrong side, omitting ribs.

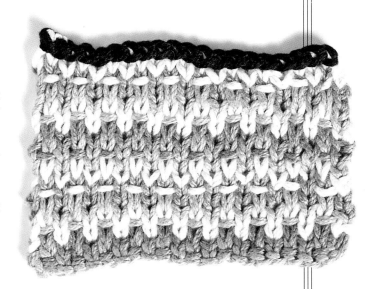

Echoes of
the Past

Jacquard and Cable Sweater

In Celtic superstition, it was believed that great spiritual benefits resulted from burial where two seas meet; thus, the narrow neck of land called the Braighe has been a notable burial ground for centuries. Its earliest monuments, erected around 1450, were for the chiefs of the Clan Macleod. I have always liked the muted colors of the stones, with their patches of lichen, and I used them in a casual sweater that combines Jacquard, Swiss darning, and double cable to create an effect of bas-relief.

RATING ● ● ● ●

Jacquard and Cable Sweater

SIZES
To fit chest 38–40/42–44in(97–102/107–112cm)

KNITTED MEASUREMENTS
Chest 45/48in(114/122cm)
Length from top of shoulder
27/28in(68.5/71cm)
Sleeve length 20½/21in(52/53.5cm)

MATERIALS
Soft-spun bulky yarn, 120yds per 2oz(98m per 50g):
11 2oz(50g) hanks in blue-gray; 2 2(50g) hanks in charcoal; 2 2oz(50g) hanks in lichen: 1 2oz(50g) hank in silver gray.
1 pair each size 8(5mm) and size 10(6mm) needles
1 circular 16in(40cm) size 8(5mm) needle.
1 cable needle
Stitch holders
8 Jacquard bobbins

GAUGE
8 sts and 10 rows to 2in(5cm) measured over st st, using size 10(6mm) needles.

Cable panel (12 sts)
Row 1 (right side): p2, k8, p2.
Row 2: k2, p8, k2.
Row 3: p2, sl next 2 sts to cn and hold at back, k2, then k2 from cn; sl next 2 sts to cn and hold at front, k2, then k2 from cn; p2.
Row 4: as row 2.
Row 5: as row 1.
Row 6: as row 2.
Rep rows 1 through 6.

BACK
With size 8(5mm) needles and blue-gray, cast on 90/94 sts. K1, p1 rib for 3/3½in(8/9cm).

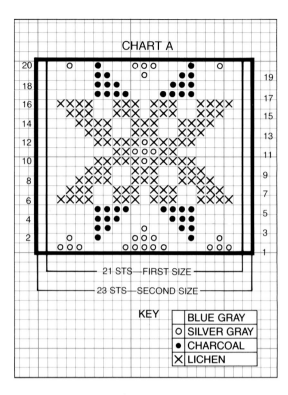

CHART A

21 STS—FIRST SIZE
23 STS—SECOND SIZE

KEY

	BLUE GRAY
O	SILVER GRAY
●	CHARCOAL
X	LICHEN

Next row—Increase
Rib 5/3, *m1, rib 4; rep from * to the last 5/3 sts; m1, rib 5/3—111/117 sts.

Fill 3 Jacquard bobbins each of charcoal and lichen (for instructions on how to make bobbins, see page xiii). **Note:** Swiss darn silver-gray stitches marked on chart A after garment pieces are completed and knit these sts in blue-gray. (For instructions on how to Swiss darn, see page xiii.)

Beg at row 1 of cable panel and chart A, patt as follows:

Work cable panel over the first 12 sts; *join in appropriate bobbin and work chart A patt over the next 21/23 sts; cable panel over the next 12 sts; rep from * to end of row.

Continue in this manner, repeating the 6 cable panel rows and the 20 chart A patt rows as set. Break off and rejoin colors on chart A patt as required. Work straight until back measures 27/28in(68.5/71cm) from beg, with right side facing for next row.

Shape shoulders

Keeping continuity of patt as far as possible, bind off 12/13 sts at beg of next 4 rows. Then bind off 13/14 sts at beg of next 2 rows. Place the rem 37 sts on a holder for back neck.

FRONT

Work as for back until front measures 25/26in(63.5/66cm), ending with right side facing for next row.

Shape neck and left shoulder

Patt the first 47/50 sts; place the next 17 sts on a holder for front neck; place the rem sts on a spare needle.

Turn, and keeping continuity of patt as far as possible, shape as follows:

Patt 1 row straight. Patt the next row and place the 2 sts at neck edge on front neck holder. Dec 1 st at neck edge of next 6 rows. Patt 1 row straight, then the dec 1 st at neck edge of next and foll alt row. **At the same time,** when front corresponds in length with back at beg of shoulder shaping, and with right side facing for next row, bind off shoulder on right-side rows as follows: bind off 12/13 sts twice; bind off the rem 13/14 sts.

Shape right neck and shoulder

With right side facing, rejoin appropriate yarns to the 47/50 sts on spare needle and, keeping continuity, patt to end of row. Then, keeping continuity of patt as far as possible, work as for left neck and shoulder, reversing shapings.

SLEEVES

With size 8(5mm) needles and blue-gray, cast on 42/44 sts. K1, p1 rib for 3in(8cm).

Next row—Increase

Rib 1/2, *m1, rib 4; rep from * to the last 1/2 sts; m1, rib 1/2—53/55 sts.

Fill 3 Jacquard bobbins each with charcoal and lichen, and 2 with silver-gray. Swiss darn silver-gray on chart A and knit in silver-gray on charts B and C.

Change to size 10(6mm) needles and patt as follows: work chart B over the first 4 sts; cable panel over the next 12 sts; chart A over the next 21/23 sts. cable panel over the next 12 sts; chart C over the last 4 sts.

Continue in this manner, repeating the 20 rows of chart A, 36 rows of charts B and C, and the 6 rows of cable panel, and inc 1 st at each end of every third row until there are 101/103 sts in total. Work charts B and C over all increased sts.

Continue straight in patts until sleeve measures 20½/21in(52/53.5cm) from beg, with right side facing for next row. Break off colors except blue-gray and bind off all sts.

FINISHING

Press all pieces lightly on wrong side, omitting ribbing.

Swiss darn silver-gray on sts as marked on chart A. Sew back and front together at shoulders and press seams lightly on wrong side.

Neckband

With right side facing, circular size 8(5mm) needle, and blue-gray, pick up and knit the 37 sts from back neck holder; knit up 13 sts to front neck holder; pick up and knit the 21 sts from front neck holder; knit up 13 sts to back neck—84 sts.

Jacquard and Cable Sweater

Double cable

Inverted turtle collar.
crew neck

Jacquard
Flowers.

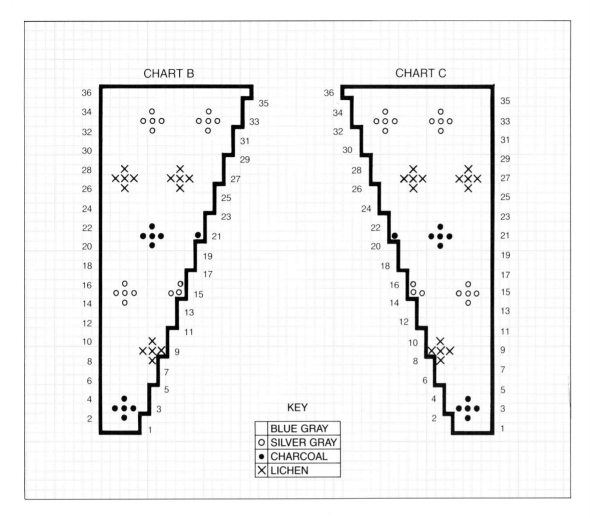

CHART B

CHART C

KEY

	BLUE GRAY
O	SILVER GRAY
•	CHARCOAL
X	LICHEN

K1, p1 rib for 8 rows. Bind off loosely and evenly in rib.

Collar

With circular size 8(5mm) needle and blue-gray, cast on 84 sts. Work rounds of k1, p1 rib for 7in(18cm). Bind off loosely and evenly in rib.

Sew bound-off edge of collar loosely to inside of neckband pickup line.

Place center top of sleeves at shoulder seams and sew sleeves to body. Press seams lightly on wrong side.

Sew up side and sleeve seams. Press seams lightly on wrong side.

Traditional Aran Gansey

The intertwining stonework on another Macleod tomb lies at the very core of Gaelic imagery and artwork. I used neither its color nor its pattern but the basic visual concept, which I believe is closely related to that of Aran knitting. Hence this Aran gansey—a strong, traditional design, and a quintessential classic.

RATING ● ● ● ●

Traditional Aran Gansey

SIZES
To fit chest
38/40/42/44in(97/102/107/112cm)

KNITTED MEASUREMENTS
Chest 43/45/47/49in(110/115/119/125cm)
Length from top of shoulder
27/27½/28/28½in(69/70/71/72.5cm)
Sleeve length
19/19½/19½/20in(48.5/49.5/49.5/51cm)

MATERIALS
24/24/24/25 1¾oz(50g) balls of standard
Aran yarn, 78yds per 1¾oz(72m per 50g)
1 pair each size 5(3¾mm) and size
8(5mm) needles
1 set of 4 double-pointed needles or circular size 6(4mm) needle
1 cable needle
Stitch holders

GAUGE
11 sts and 13 rows to 2in(5cm) measured
over moss stitch, using size 8(5mm)
needles.

PATTERN PANELS
Moss stitch (even no. of sts)
Rows 1 & 2: *k1, p1; rep from * to end.
Rows 3 & 4: *p1, k1; rep from * to end.
Rep rows 1 through 4.

Wishbone cable (10 sts)
Row 1 (wrong side): k2, p6, k2.
Row 2: p2, k2, sl2 purlwise with yarn at
back, k2, p2.
Row 3: k2, p2, sl2 purlwise with yarn at
front, p2, k2.
Row 4: p2, sl next 2 sts to cn and hold at
back, k1, then k2 from cn; sl next st to cn
and hold at front, k2, then k1 from cn; p2.
Rep rows 1 through 4.

Fivefold braid (18 sts)
Row 1 & all wrong-side rows: k2, (p2,
k1) 4 times, p2, k2.
Row 2: p2, (k2, p1) 4 times, k2, p2.
Row 4: p2, k2, (p1, sl next 3 sts to cn and
hold at front, k2, then sl the p st back to left
needle and p it, k2 from cn) twice; p2.
Row 6: as row 2.
Row 8: p2, (sl next 3 sts to cn and hold at
back, k2, then sl the p st back to left needle
and p it, k2 from cn, p1) twice; k2, p2.
Rep rows 1 through 8.

Honeycomb (multiples of 8 plus 4)
Row 1 & all wrong-side rows: k2, p to
the last 2 sts of panel, k2.
Row 2: p2, *sl next 2 sts to cn and hold at
back, k2, then k2 from cn (back cross—
bc); sl next 2 sts to cn and hold at front, k2,
then k2 from cn (front cross—fc); rep from
* to last 2 sts of panel, p2.
Row 4: p2, k to the last 2 sts of panel, p2.
Row 6: p2, *fc, bc; rep from * to the last 2
sts of panel, p2.
Row 8: as row 4.
Rep rows 1 through 8.

BACK
With size 5(3¾mm) needles, cast on
116/126/126/136 sts and work cabled rib
as follows:
Row 1 (right side): *p2, k2, p2, k4; rep
from * to the last 6 sts; p2, k2, p2.
Row 2: * k2, p2, k2, p4; rep from * to the
last 6 sts; k2, p2, k2.
Row 3: * p2, k2, p2, sl next 2 sts to cn and
hold at front, k2, then k2 from cn; rep from
* to the last 6 sts; p2, k2, p2.
Row 4: as row 2.
Rep rows 1 through 4 until rib measures
2¾in(7cm), with right side facing for next
row.

Next row—Increase
K11/13/13/14, *m1, k3/4/3/4; rep from * to
the last 12/13/14/14 sts; m1, k12/13/14/
14—148/152/160/164 sts.

Change to size 8(5mm) needles and patt as
follows:

Work moss stitch over the first 14/16/20/22 sts; wishbone cable over the next 10 sts; fivefold braid over the next 18 sts; wishbone cable over the next 10 sts; honeycomb over the next 44 sts; wishbone cable over the next 10 sts; fivefold braid over the next 18 sts; wishbone cable over the next 10 sts; moss stitch over the last 14/16/20/22 sts.

Continue in this manner until back measures 25/25½/26/26½in(64/65/66/67.5cm) from beg, with right side facing for next row.

Right shoulder
Bind off the first 26/28/32/34 sts, then continue to bind off, decreasing as follows:

(K2tog, and continue to bind off, binding off 4 sts) twice, then k2tog and continue to bind off, binding off 3 sts. Bind off the next 7 sts.

Back neck
K the next 7 st, (k2tog, k3) 8 times, k7. Place these 46 sts on a holder for back neck.

Left shoulder
Bind off the next 10 sts, (k2tog, and continue to bind off, binding off 4 sts) twice, then k2tog, and continue binding off the rem sts.

FRONT
Work as for back until front measures 23¾/24¼/24¾/25¼in(60.5/61.5/63/64cm)—i.e., to within 8 rows of back length—with right side facing for next row.

Left front shoulder
Patt the first 50/52/56/58 sts, k2tog. Place the rem sts on a spare needle.

Keeping continuity of patt panels, work the 51/53/57/59 sts of left shoulder, decreasing 1 st at neck edge of next and every foll alt row until 47/49/53/55 sts rem. Bind off sts as for back right shoulder.

Front neck
With right side facing, rejoin yarn and work the next 44 sts (center front) as follows: p2, (k2tog, k3) 8 times, p2. Place these 36 sts on a holder for front neck.

Right front shoulder
K2tog, patt the rem 50/52/56/58 sts. Keeping continuity of patt panels, work the 51/53/57/59 sts of left front shoulder as for right front shoulder. Bind off sts as for back left shoulder.

RIGHT SLEEVE
With size 5(3¾mm) needles, cast on 56/60/60/64 sts and rib as follows:

First size
Rib as for back for 2¾in(7cm), with right side facing for next row.

Second and third sizes
Rib as for back, but omit the first and last 3 sts on every row. Work for 2¾in(7cm), with right side facing for next row.

Fourth size
Rib as for back, but omit the first and last st on every row. Work for 2¾in(7cm), with right side facing for next row.

Next row—Increase
First size: *m1, k5; rep from * to the last st; m1, k1—68 sts.
Second and third sizes: k2, *m1, k5; rep from * to the last 3 sts; m1, k3—72 sts.
Fourth size: k4, *m1, k5; rep from * to end of row—76 sts.

Traditional Aran Gansey

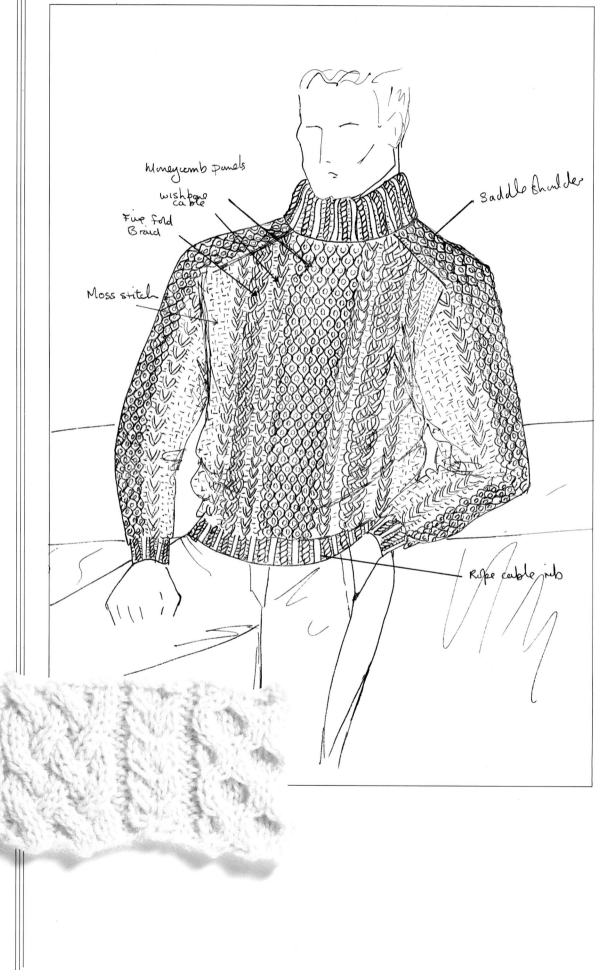

Honeycomb panels

wishbone cable

Fine fold Braid

Moss stitch

Saddle shoulder

Rope cable ribs

122

All sizes

Change to size 8(5mm) needles and patt as follows: work moss stitch over the first 10/12/12/14 sts; wishbone cable over the next 10 sts; honeycomb over the next 28 sts; wishbone cable over the next 10 sts; moss stitch over the last 10/12/12/14 sts.

Continue in this manner and inc 1 st at each end of the fourth/sixth/second/eighth row, and thereafter at each end of every fourth row, until there are 116/120/122/124 sts in total. Work all increased sts in moss stitch. Continue straight in patt until sleeve measures 19/19½/19½/20in (48.5/49.5/49.5/51cm) from beg, with right side facing for next row.

Saddle

Bind off the first 44/46/47/48 sts, patt to end of row.

Next row: bind off the first 44/46/47/48 sts, patt the rem 28 sts.

Keeping continuity of patt, continue working the 28 sts of honeycomb until saddle corresponds in length with bound-off edge of right front shoulder, with wrong side facing for next row. Shape saddle top as follows:

Next row: patt 22 sts, place the rem sts on a holder.

Row 2: keeping continuity, patt 22 sts.
Row 3: patt 14 sts, place the rem 8 sts on same holder.
Row 4: keeping continuity, patt 14 sts and place all sts on same holder.

LEFT SLEEVE

Work as for right sleeve, but working saddle until it corresponds in length with bound-off edge of left front shoulder, with **right** side facing for next row. Then shape saddle top as for right sleeve.

FINISHING

Do not press garment pieces.

Sew sides of left sleeve saddle to bound-off edges of back and front left shoulder. Sew sides of right sleeve saddle to bound-off edges of back and front right shoulder.

Press seams very lightly on the wrong side.

Collar

With double-pointed set or circular size 6(4mm) needles, pick up and knit the 46 sts from back neck holder; pick up and knit the sts from left saddle holder as follows: k2, (k2tog, k2) 6 times, k2. Knit up 7 sts to front neck holder; pick up and knit the 36 sts from front neck holder; knit up 7 sts to right saddle holder; pick up and knit the sts of right saddle as for left—140 sts total.

Turn garment inside out so that collar will be worked on the wrong side, and patt as follows:
Rounds 1 & 2: *p2, k2, p2, k4; rep from * to end of round.
Round 3: *p2, k2, p2, sl 2 sts to cn and hold at front, k2, then k2 from cn; rep from * to end of round.
Round 4: as rounds 1 & 2.

Rep rounds 1 through 4 until collar measures 6½in(16.5cm). Bind off evenly.

Sew bound-off edges of sleeves to body. Press seams very lightly on wrong side. Sew up side and sleeve seams. Press seams very lightly on wrong side.

Aran Cardigan

The Callanish stone circle on the west coast of Lewis is the ultimate echo from the past. This ancient neolithic circle is about 5,000 years old, and experts are still arguing over its astronomical significance. From a few feet away, some of the stones seem patterned by hand, but closer examination reveals the work of wind and rain over thousands of years. It is this texture alone that I sought to capture in a modern development of the Aran theme. The panels on this casual, country cardigan are set in the traditional Aran way, but the style is not, and the patterns, although Aran style, are contemporary.

RATING ● ● ● ●

Aran Cardigan

SIZES
To fit chest 38–40/42–44in(97–102/107–112cm)

KNITTED MEASUREMENTS
Chest (buttoned)
47½/51½in(121/131cm)
Length from top of shoulder
29/30in(74/76cm)
Sleeve length 20/20½in(51/52cm)

MATERIALS
13/14 3½oz(100g) hanks of Aran wool,
164yds per 3½oz(150m per 100g)
1 pair each size 6(4mm) and size 8(5mm)
needles
1 cable needles
2 stitch holders
Stitch markers
6 buttons

GAUGE
19 sts and 26 rows to 4in(10cm), measured over **panel E** patt, using size 8(5mm) needles (cast on 37 sts and work swatch as first size **panel E**).

Pattern panels
Panel A
Row 1 (right side): (p3, k1) 3/4 times, p3.
Row 2: (k3, p1) 3/4 times, k3.
Row 3: (p3, k into front, back, then front of next st) 3/4 times, p3.
Row 4: (k3, p3tog) 3/4 times, k3.
Rep rows 1 through 4.

Panel B
Row 1 (right side): k1b, p1, k4, p1, k1b.
Row 2: p1b, k1, p4, k1, p1b.
Row 3: k1b, p1; sl 2 sts to cn and hold at front, k2 then k2 from cn; p1, k1b.
Row 4: as row 2.
Row 5: as row 1.
Row 6: as row 2.
Rep rows 1 through 6.

Panel C
Row 1 (right side): p3, k4, p4, k4, p3.
Row 2: k3, p4, k4 p4, k3.
Row 3: p3; sl next 2 sts to cn and hold at front, k2, then k2 from cn; p4; sl next 2 sts to cn and hold at back, k2, then k2 from cn; p3.
Rows 4, 6, 8, & 10: as row 2.
Row 5: p3, k4, p1; make bobble thus— (k1, p1, k1) into *each* of the next 2 sts, turn and p6, turn and k1, ssk, k2tog, k1, turn and p2tog twice, turn and k2, completing bobble; p1, k4, p3.
Row 7: as row 3.
Row 9: as row 1.
Row 11: p1, (sl2 sts to cn and hold at back, k2, then p2 from cn; s1 next 2 sts to cn and hold at front, p2, then k2 from cn) twice, p1.
Rows 12 & 14: k1, p2, k4, p4, k4, p2, k1.
Row 13: p1, k2, p4, k4, p4, k2, p1.
Row 15: p1 (sl next 2 sts to cn and hold at front, p2, then k2 from cn; sl next 2 sts to cn and hold at back, k2, then p2 from cn) twice, p1.
Row 16: as row 2.
Rep rows 1 through 16.

Panel D
Work as for panel B but instead of "hold at front" read "hold at back."

Panel E
Row 1 (right side): p2/3, (k1, p3) 8 times, k1, p2/3.
Row 2: k2/3, (p1, k3) 8 times, p1, k2/3.
Row 3: p2/3, (k into front, back, then front of next st, p3) 8 times, k into front, back, then front of next st, p2/3.
Row 4: k2/3, (p3tog, k3) 8 times, p3tog, k2/3.
Rep rows 1 through 4.

Panel F
Row 1 (right side): p1, (k1, p3) 3 times, k1, p2/3.
Row 2: k2/3, (p1, k3) 3 times, p1, k1.
Row 3: p1, (k into front, back, then front of next st, p3) 3 times, k into front, back, then front of next st, p2/3.
Row 4: k2/3, (p3tog, k3) 3 times, p3tog, k1.
Rep rows 1 through 4.

Panel G

Row 1 (right side): p2/3, (k1, p3) 3 times, k1, p1.

Row 2: k1, p1, (k3, p1) 3 times, k2/3.

Row 3: p2/3, (k into front, back, then front of next st, p3) 3 times, k into front, back, then front of next st, p1.

Row 4: k1, (p3tog, k3) 3 times, p3tog, k2/3.

Rep rows 1 through 4.

BACK

With size 6(4mm) needles, cast on 112/122 sts. K1, p1 rib for 3½in(9cm).

Next row—Increase

Rib 1/6, *m1, rib 5; rep from * to the last 1/6 sts; m1, rib 1/6—135/145 sts.

Change to size 8(5mm) needles and patt as follows: work **panel A** over the first 15/19 sts; **panel B** over the next 8 sts; **panel C** over the next 18 sts; **panel D** over the next 8 sts; **panel E** over the next 37/39 sts; **panel B** over the next 8 sts; **panel C** over the next 18 sts; **panel D** over the next 8 sts; **panel A** over the last 15/19 sts.

Continue working pattern panels as set until back measures 18/18½in(46/47cm) from beg. Place a marker at each end of row to mark armholes, then continue as set until armholes measure 11/11½in(28/29cm), with right side facing for next row.

Shape shoulders

Keeping continuity of patt, bind off 16/17 sts at beg of next 2 rows.

Bind off 16/17 sts at beg of next 2 rows, knitting tog fourth and fifth sts of rope cable, and fifth and sixth sts of bobble cable panel during bind-off.

Bind off 16/18 sts at beg of next 2 rows, knitting tog thirteenth and fourteenth sts of bobble cable panel, and fourth and fifth sts of rope cable during bind-off.

Bind off the rem 39/41 st (back neck).

POCKET LININGS (MAKE TWO)

With size 6(4mm) needles, cast on 34 sts and st st for 6in(15cm). Place sts on a spare needle.

RIGHT FRONT

†With size 6(4mm) needles, cast on 54/58 sts. K1, p1 rib for 3½in(9cm).

Next row—Increase

Rib 2/1, *m1, rib 5; rep from * to the last 2 sts; m1, rib 2—65/70 sts.††

Change to size 8(5mm) needles and patt as follows: work **panel F** over the first 16/17 sts; **panel B** over the next 8 sts; **panel C** over the next 18 sts; **panel D** over the next 8 sts; **panel A** over the last 15/19 sts.

Continue working pattern panels as set for 6in(15cm), with right side facing for next row.

Make pocket opening & place lining

Patt 16/17 sts as set; place the next 34 sts on a holder and work row 1 of **panel B**, row 9 of **panel C**, and row 1 of **panel D** over the 34 sts of one pocket lining; patt the rem 15/19 sts as set.

Continue working pattern panels as set until front measures 14½in(37cm) from beg, with right side facing for next row.

Shape front neckline

Keeping continuity of patt, dec 1 st at beg of next, and then at same edge of every foll fifth row until 48/52 sts rem. **At the same time,** when front corresponds in length with back at armhole, place a marker at armhole edge.

Continue straight in patt until front corresponds in length with back at beg of shoulder shaping, with wrong side facing for next row.

Shape shoulder

Bind off 16/17 sts and, keeping continuity, patt to end of row. Patt 1 row straight, then bind off 16/17 sts at beg of next row, knitting tog fourth and fifth sts of rope cable, and fifth and sixth sts of bobble cable panel during bind-off; patt to end of row. Patt 1 row straight, then bind off the rem 16/18 sts, knitting tog thirteenth and fourteenth sts of bobble cable panel, and fourth and fifth sts of rope cable during bind-off.

Aran Cardigan

Aran Cardigan
Dropped Shoulders, front pockets

sizes 38/40/42/44 in

128

LEFT FRONT

Work as for right front from † to ††.

Change to size 8(5mm) needles and patt as follows: work **panel A** over the first 15/19 sts; **panel D** over the next 8 sts; **panel C** over the next 18 sts; **panel B** over the next 8 sts; **panel G** over the last 16/17 sts.

Continue working pattern panels as set for 6in(15cm), with right side facing for next row.

Make pocket opening and place lining

Patt 15/19 sts as set; place the next 34 sts on a holder and work row 1 of **panel D,** row 9 of **panel C,** and row 1 of **panel B** over the 34 sts of rem pocket lining; patt the rem 16/17 sts as set.

Continue working pattern panels as set until front measures 14½in(37cm), with right side facing for next row.

Shape front neckline

Dec 1 st at end of next row. Keeping continuity of patt, dec 1 st at same edge of every foll fifth row until 48/52 sts rem. **At the same time,** when front corresponds in length with back at armhole, place a marker at armhole edge. Continue in patt until front corresponds in length with back at beg of shoulder shaping, and with right side facing for next row, shape shoulder as for right front.

SLEEVES (MAKE 2)

With size 6(4mm) needles, cast on 52/54 sts. K1, p1 rib for 3in(8cm).

Next row—increase

Rib 4/5, *m1, rib 4; rep from * to the last 4/5 sts; m1, rib 4/5—64/66 sts.

Change to size 8(5mm) needles and patt as follows: work **panel A—first size/panel F—first size** over the first 15/16 sts; **panel B** over the next 8 sts; **panel C** over the next 18 sts; **panel D** over the next 8 sts; **panel A—first size/panel G—first size** over the last 15/16 sts.

Continue working pattern panels as set and inc 1 st at each end of third row. Then inc 1 st at each end of every foll fourth row until there are 114/116 sts in total. Work all increased sts into patt.

Continue straight in patt until sleeve measures 20/20½in(51/52 cm) from beg. Bind off all sts, knitting tog fourth and fifth sts of rope cables, and sixth and seventh sts and thirteenth and fourteenth sts of bobble cable panel, during bind-off.

FINISHING

Do not press garment pieces.

Slip stitch pocket linings to fronts.

Pocket rib

With size 6(4mm) needles, knit across the 34 sts of pocket opening, knitting tog fourth and fifth sts of rope cables, and ninth and tenth sts of bobble cable panel—31 sts rem. K1, p1 rib for 1in(2.5cm). Bind off evenly in rib.

Stitch ends of pocket ribs to fronts.

Sew back and fronts at shoulder seams. Press seams very lightly on wrong side. Place center top of sleeves at shoulder seams, and sew sleeves to body between markers. Press seams very lightly on wrong side.

Sew up side and sleeve seams and press seams very lightly on wrong side.

Button Band

With size 6(4mm) needles, cast on 11 sts.
Row 1 (right side): k2, (p1, k1) 4 times, k1.
Row 2: k1, (p1, k1) 5 times.
Rep these 2 rows until band fits up right front and around to center back neck when slightly stretched. Sew in place as you go along. Bind off in rib.

Mark position of 6 buttons on button border with pins, first to come 1in(2.5cm) from lower edge, last to come at beg of neckline shaping, and rem spaced evenly between.

Buttonhole band

Work as button band with the addition of 6 buttonholes placed to correspond with pins on button band. **To make buttonholes:** (right side) rib 4, bind off 3, rib to end and back, casting on 3 sts over those bound off.

Sew up band at center back neck. Sew on buttons.

Yarn Information

YARNS USED IN PHOTOGRAPHED SWEATERS

Gansey Style Sweater, p. 4
Silk City Fibers:
Fiorella 100% lambswool in navy
Cocoon 100% silk in white

Fair Isle Vest, p. 10
Jamieson & Smith's Shetland 2-ply jumper weight:
202 fawn
142 petrol blue
FC8 rust
FC39 blue mix
1288 deep coral mix
FC43 corn
118 green

Anchor Waistcoat, p.14
Rowan Silkstones:
marble, blue mist, natural, mulled wine, woad, and chilli

Boat and Rope Sweater, p. 20
Jamieson & Smith's Shetland 3-ply:
H1 white
H25 pale blue
H47 bright blue

Classic Cardigan, p. 26
Rowan Fine Fleck Tweed:
54 dark green
100 soft green
51 blue
64 gray

Sand Rib Vest, p. 32
Silk City Fibers Silkenwool:
shade no. A

Rock and Sand Sweater, p. 36
Jamieson & Smith's Shetland 3-ply:
H3a light fawn
H3 dark fawn
H42 old gold mix
H23 blue-gold mix
H6 green-gold mix

Sand Stitch Cotton Sweater, p. 42
Crystal Palace Yarns:
Georgia Cotton

Check Rock Sweater, p. 48
Silk City Fibers Silkenwool:
19 dark green
03 blue
B beige
07 purple
88 dark blue
82 dusky pink
01 pale turquoise

Textured Multicolor Sweater, p. 54
Irene Preston Miller's hand-dyed wool:
Mauve and complimentary multicolored yarn

Mohair Sweater, p. 60
Standard mohair yarn:
claret
midnight blue
dark navy

Check Stitch Sweater, p. 66
Jamieson & Smith's Embo 3-ply wool:
shade no. 3020

Textured Chevron Sweater, p. 72
Rowan Sandy Black Twist:
natural
gray
charcoal

Mohair Cardigan, p. 78
Standard mohair yarn:
dark navy
dusk blue
cloud gray
honey gold
light lemon

Norwegian Style Sweater, p. 84
Rowan Fleck DK:
shade no. 62F
Rowan Designer DK:
shade numbers: 638, 641, 640, 125,
63, 647

Moss Rib Sweater, p. 90
Crystal Palace Yarns:
Carnival 100% wool, color no. 323

Shawl Collar Sweater, p. 96
Crystal Palace Yarns:
Kaleidoscope, color no. 1010

Openwork Cotton Sweater, p. 100
Crystal Palace Yarns:
Biwa Mercerized Pearl Cotton,
shade no. 9709

Cotton Raglan Sweater, p. 106
Crystal Palace Yarns Monterey Mercerized
Cotton:
000 natural
84 gray
083 sand
020 black

Jacquard and Cable Sweater, p. 112
Jamieson & Smith's 2-ply Soft Spun:
BSS4 blue-gray
BSS13 charcoal
BSS26 lichen
BSS17 silver-gray

Traditional Aran Gansey, p. 118
Standard Aran yarn

Aran Cardigan, p.124
Rowan Aran:
natural

YARN SUPPLIERS

Crystal Palace Yarns
3006 San Pablo Avenue
Berkeley, California 94702

Jamieson & Smith
Tomato Factory Yarn Company
8 Church St.
Lambertville, NJ 08530

Irene Preston Miller
P.O. Box 135
Croton-on-Hudson, New York 10520

Rowan Yarns
Tomato Factory Yarn Company
8 Church St.
Lambertville, NJ 08530

Silk City Fibers
155 Oxford Street
Paterson, New Jersey 07522

About the Author

Alice Starmore is a designer, author, and teacher who began knitting at the age of four. She began knitting professionally in 1976 and two years later received a Winston Churchill Travelling Fellowship, which enabled her to travel for two months throughout Norway, Sweden, and Finland to collect traditional knitting patterns.

In 1985, Alice was invited to teach at the first Knitting Guild of America National Convention, held in Dallas. Her classes were so successful that she has taught at every K.G.A. National Convention since then. She has also completed several nationwide teaching tours in the United States. Although her reputation in the United States is that of an expert on traditional hand knitting, Alice is also highly experienced in machine knitting and is an industrial consultant in that field.

Her previous books include *Scandinavian Knitwear*, *Knitting from the British Islands*, *Children's Knitting from Many Lands*, and *Alice Starmore's Book of Fair Isle Knitting*. Born on the Isle of Lewis, Scotland, Alice lives there with her family.